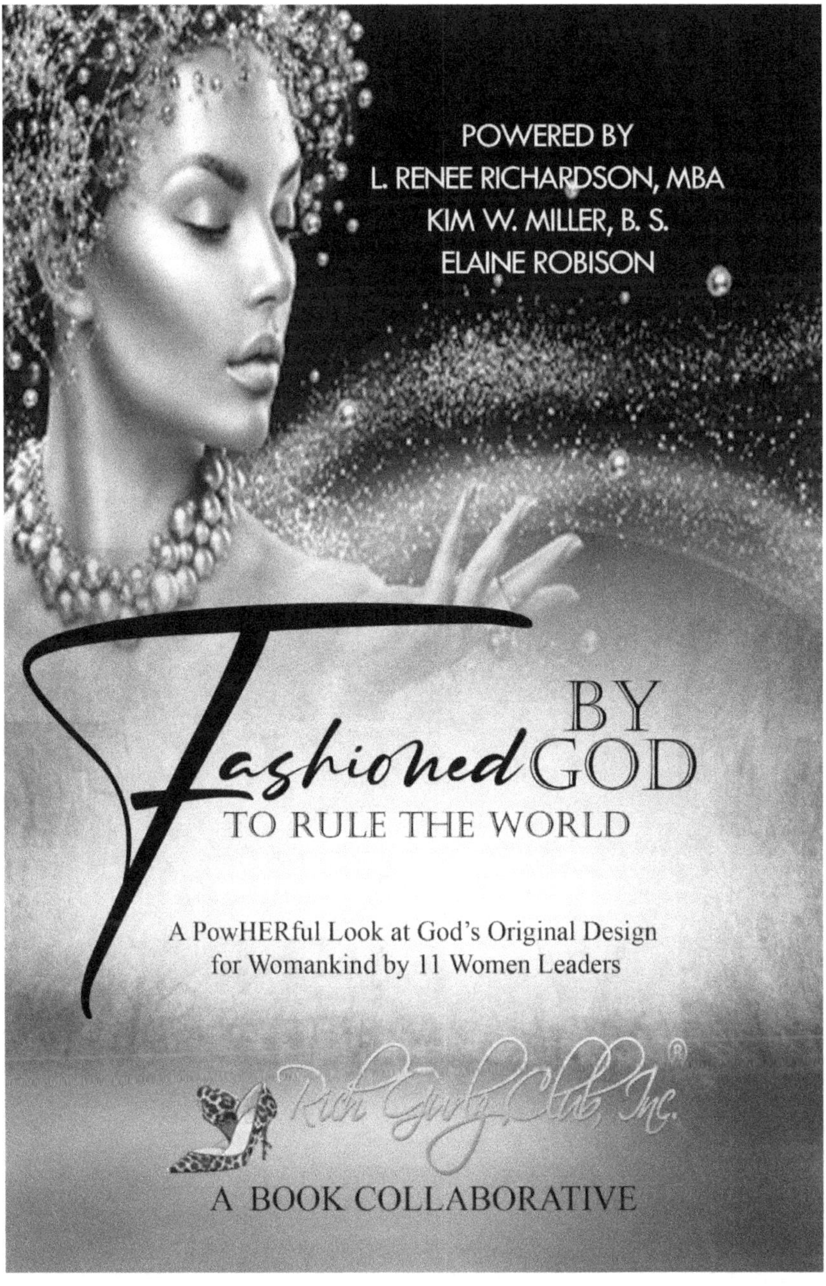

POWERED BY
L. RENEE RICHARDSON, MBA
KIM W. MILLER, B. S.
ELAINE ROBISON

Fashioned BY GOD
TO RULE THE WORLD

A PowHERful Look at God's Original Design
for Womankind by 11 Women Leaders

Rich Gurly Club, Inc.®

A BOOK COLLABORATIVE

Fashioned by God to Rule the World

A PowHERful Look at God's Original Design for Womankind by 11 Women Leaders

A Rich Gurlz Club Book Collaborative

CERTIFIED BY
WBENC/WEConnect INTERNATIONAL

WOMEN OWNED™

WWW.WOMENOWNEDLOGO.COM

Fashioned by God to Rule the World
A Message from the Founder and Publisher
L. Renee Richardson, MBA

Welcome to the Rich Gurlz Club!

Dear Rich Gurlz®,

My calling is to empower women business owners to "Pursue Your Dreams with Passion" and "Dream in Billions!"

The Rich Gurlz Club was birthed in 2016 when I was not able to find another six-figure job, so I decided to follow my heart and create my own company. Rich Gurlz is a global network of Christian women business owners, corporate executives, and ministry leaders. As Proverbs 31-inspired women we share our wealth, influence, and resources to empower others. It is our desire to protect and change laws to reflect our Father's purpose for women and take Christ to the nations.

For more than two decades we have underwritten Women of Vision and Destiny Ministries Worldwide, Inc. and, most recently, the I Am Worth It Foundation. A portion of every dollar we earn sponsors causes for women and young ladies. Our goal is to raise one dollar for every woman on the planet—a total of $4 billion.

Fashioned by God to Rule the World

Last year, during racial turmoil in the US, I launched The Rich Color Gurlz Club to serve women of color. I want to encourage women to live beyond the boundaries of ethnicity and focus on excellence in business. I know that this is possible with the Lord's leading because of my own experience.

In my prior career, I became the third highest-ranking woman of color at a company of 3,500 people by using principles of prayer, strategic planning, and excellence. They say, "nice girls do not get the corner office," but I did. I was featured in numerous magazines and publications for my stellar career. And I want to see the same happen for you!

If you would like to become a Rich Gurlz Club collaborative author, visit RichGurlzAuthors.eventbrite.com to learn more. If you would like to book one of our Rich Gurlz authors as a speaker at your conference or event speaker, contact our Columbus, GA office at (404) 797-3071.

It is my prayer that the messages in this book, and the phenomenal women who contributed to it, encourage you to reach beyond your perceived limitations to achieve excellence in every area of your life.

Warmly,

L. Renee Richardson

Dedication

This Rich Gurlz Club Book Collaborative is dedicated to every woman on the planet with big, bodacious, and brilliant dreams. We believe that the world is waiting on you to leave your legacy and impact other women. We pray that you are inspired to discover what God has put inside of you and live your rich, big dreams today!

#iruletheworld

A Letter from our Signature Author
Kim W. Miller, BA

Dear Reader,

I am overwhelmed and delighted with the thought that God made and fashioned me. God has always had, and continues to have, superb thoughts about you and me! I'm grateful that we were appointed to deliver this masterpiece, *Fashioned by God to Rule the World,* to all of you. It has been a distinct honor and an amazing opportunity to be aligned with such a fabulous, creative and talented group of authors who were used as vessels and messengers for this assignment.

What a powerful realization we have in knowing we have been fashioned by God to rule our world. Through my writing and editing experience on this project, the world of God's authority, with which we all have been empowered to rule, has been unveiled to me, as well as my fellow sisters. Knowing this truth, there is no longer room in our lives for nagging doubts, fear or inferiority. We all have regained our "Genesis" consciousness to walk, talk, think, believe, know and live in the authority of ruling the world as God intended from the very beginning of time.

It is the desire of each author who has contributed to this project that after reading this book you will shine with the realization that, in fact, you are made and *Fashioned by God to Rule the World*.

I encourage you to consume every word and enjoy journeying with us!

Sincerely,
Kim W. Miller

A Letter from our Signature Author
Elaine Robison

Dear Reader,

To God be the Glory for the things that He has done, what He is doing and what He is going to do. Who would have ever thought that I would be a collective co-author, writing a book with some powerful women as we discover together how we have been *Fashioned by God to Rule the World*?

This book was not in my plans, but God had a plan for me to interweave my personal story of loss and redemption into the story of Eve, the first woman to lose a child. I was told after I lost my daughter that I needed to write about my experiences so that I would never forget the mighty miracles that happened during her illness, her death and afterward. I can say for sure that the awesomeness of God has kept me from that time until now.

I pray that all of the chapters will uplift, encourage, empower and give hope to those who may read this book. What I know is that God didn't allow the death of my child to destroy me. The enemy meant it for evil, but God gets all of the glory out of it. He taught me that there is life after the loss of a child. As it was with Eve, God blessed me and caused me to smile again. Eve had another son, Seth, and she felt that God had given her another son in place of Abel.

God also blessed me with many more children. I will never forget my daughter, but today I'm not dying, I am thriving in Him.

Be blessed!

Sincerely,
Elaine Robison

Fashioned by God to Rule the World

Copyright ©2021 by Wealth and Riches Today. All rights reserved. Written permission must be secured from the publisher to use or reproduce any part of this book, except for brief quotations in critical reviews or articles. If you would like to use material from this book (other than for review purposes), prior written permission must be obtained by contacting the publisher.

Published in Chicago, Illinois by Wealth and Riches Today
John Hancock Center
875 North Michigan
31st Floor
Chicago, IL 60611

Rich Gurlz Club is a wholly owned subsidiary of
Wealth and Riches Today, Inc. Chicago, IL.
Office: 404.797.3071
Email: lrenee.richardson@wealthandrichestoday.com

Rich Gurlz Club Today titles may be purchased in bulk for educational, business, fundraising, or sales promotional use. Email lrenee.richardson@wealthandrichestoday.com for further information.

Unless otherwise noted, all Scripture quotations are taken from the Holy Bible, KING JAMES VERSION®. Copyright© 1982 by Thomas Nelson, Inc. Used by permission. All rights reserved.

Scripture quotations marked NKJV are taken from the Holy Bible, NEW KING JAMES VERSION®. Copyright© 1982 by Thomas Nelson, Inc. Used by permission. All rights reserved.

Fashioned by God to Rule the World

Scriptures marked NIV are taken from the NEW INTERNATION AL VERSION (NIV): Scripture taken from THE HOLY BIBLE,

NEW INTERNATIONAL VERSION ®. Copyright©1973, 1978, 1984, 2011 by Biblica, Inc.™. Used by permission of Zondervan.

Scriptures marked AMP are taken from the AMPLIFIED BIBLE (AMP): Scripture taken from the AMPLIFIED® BIBLE, Copyright © 1954, 1958, 1962, 1964, 1965, 1987 by the Lockman Foundation Used by Permission. (www.Lockman.org)

While the author has made every effort to provide accurate Internet addresses at the time of publication, neither the publisher nor the author assumes any responsibility for errors or for changes that occur after publication.

ISBN: 978-1-7366619-8

Library of Congress Cataloging in Publication

2021 first edition

Rich Gurlz Club, Inc.®

CHICAGO \\ ATLANTA \\ NEW YORK \\ CAPE TOWN

Fashioned by God to Rule the World

To_____

From_____

Special Note

_____

_____

_____

_____

TABLE OF CONTENTS

Fashioned by God to Rule the World

Chapter 1: The PowHER to Create
(Genesis 1:1-2)
Faith Thomas

Chapter 2: The PowHER of Light in Innovation
(Genesis 1:3-5)
Erica Holmes

Chapter 3: The Seasons of a Woman's Life
(Genesis 1:14)
Barbara Ellzey

Chapter 4: RulHERship for Women
(Genesis 1:26-28,31)
Sheriolyn Curry

Chapter 5: The PowHER of Holy Rest and Spa
(Genesis 2:1-2)
Corine Carter Murphy

Chapter 6: Wealth Creation in the Garden
(Genesis 2:8-14)
L. Renee Richardson

Chapter 7: The Suitable Wife
(Genesis 2:18)
Kim Coleman

Fashioned by God to Rule the World

Chapter 8: The Woman's Enemy
(Genesis 3:1)
Crystal Wilhoite

Chapter 9: The PowHER of Focus: Overcoming Distraction
(Genesis 3:5-6)
Saneeta Golden

Chapter 10: Eve: First Lady of the Universe
(Genesis 3:20)
Kim W. Miller

Chapter 11: The Loss of a Child
(Genesis 4:8)
Elaine Robison

Genesis 1:28b
God blessed them and said to them, "Have many children. Fill the earth and take control of it. Rule over the fish in the sea and the birds of the air. Rule over every living thing that moves on the earth."

Fashioned by God to Rule the World

Chapter 1
The PowHer to Create

Faith Thomas, Med, MACC-SLP

Faith's HERstory

My name is Faith, and I am the proud mother of two wonderful children, Meadow Imani and Chace Montgomery Sherrod. I count motherhood as a blessing and a joy; however, I do not take my role as a mom lightly. Bringing both of my children into the world was not easy for me compared to some others, but I thank God that I am healed and whole.

I was born in South Carolina and raised in a rural area called Islandton. It's about forty miles from Beaufort, South Carolina and roughly fifty miles from Charleston in the opposite direction. I am the youngest child and only girl born to Raul and Gloria Bradley. Growing up in a house full of boys, I was a prissy tomboy. I climbed trees in a dress, played football in a skirt, and ran as fast as the boys. Both of my parents are retired educators from the South Carolina Public School system. My dad and mom have been in ministry for as long as I can remember. My father founded a church and has pastored for over forty years; my mother's missionary ministry supported his leadership. I learned so much about serving, giving, supporting, and maintaining a relationship with God and man from my parents.

Fashioned by God to Rule the World

    I remember attending Sunday School in my living room since I was three or four years old. By the time I was eight, I was an active junior missionary. I would travel with my mom to homes belonging to members of the church and community. If she washed dishes and prayed, I helped wash and prayed. If she cleaned the bathroom and prayed, I helped clean and prayed. In addition to a comprehensive Bible class, my dad would hold healing and prayer services where I witnessed miracles happen right in front of me. He and my mother both would travel to pray, teach, provide shelter, give food, and impart the life of God to people. The giving, supporting, pouring into others, and praying what they modeled is a big part of who I am today.

    Growing up in rural South Carolina, education was especially important, and was taught as the foundation and pathway to greatness. I graduated from high school in the top ten percent of my class and went on to complete my Bachelor and Master of Arts degrees in Speech Language Pathology, as well as a Master of Education degree. I hold active licenses in South Carolina, North Carolina, and Texas, and I have worked in schools, rehabilitation centers, skilled nursing facilities, hospitals, and home health settings. Roles that I have held include a direct hire, contractor, and supervisor, as well as a manager in different work settings. In June 2017, I stepped out on faith and opened a private Speech Pathology practice. As I have worked to build my practice, the vision has expanded to target an underserved population reaching as many people as possible.

Chapter 1
The PowHER to Create

In the beginning God created the Heaven and the Earth. And the earth was without form, and void; and darkness was upon the face of the deep. And the Spirit of God moved upon the face of the waters.

—Genesis 1:1-2

In my interpretation, this beginning that the Bible speaks of, when God created the heaven and earth, He started from the height and pinnacle of nothingness. There was no form, just void and darkness. God started earth and heaven from what our minds can hardly conceive, from a blank, empty, and unidentified atmosphere. The Word goes on to explain that the Spirit of God moved upon the face of the waters. God's Spirit alone created everything that was needed for us to lead and exist in authority.

As a woman that can be extremely difficult to process, as we enjoy knowing concrete steps, expectations and order. Just like it was "in the beginning..." the power to create is always present, and it is renewed for us with each new path on this journey of life. However, God does things differently than we do, and in order to create we must learn His ways and walk in excellence.

God fashioned us from nothing into all that He created us to be while we were yet in our mother's womb. We can examine the period of creation and compare it to how God allows life to come forth. There is no light or form in a mother's womb, yet babies are conceived, grow, and develop in darkness. We have been fashioned by God and wired to rule and carry authority in the world. Just thinking of this truth brings me so much joy. God loves me that much. And He loves us all enough that we must accept the life purpose He gave us before birth, and walk in it unapologetically. Our purpose and individuality give us a specific job in the world for kingdom purposes.

How We are Fashioned

God's presence, from the time He fashions our mere existence, is evident in each stage of how we develop in our mother's womb. One of the most intricate and dynamic systems that controls much of our body is the central nervous system. It is formed in the preliminary stages of development, shortly after conception. The central nervous system is made up of the brain and spinal cord. The brain integrates information and coordinates and influences the activity of all parts of the body.

Imagine that. From conception, God placed thoughts in your brain from pre-birth that would cause you to walk a path toward ruling the world today. Moreover, God has specifically designed women in a position of authority with the ability to nurture, carry, and birth life. The child carried in the mother's womb is set for life, yet doctors are not able to tell the child's gender at this point. It is God who determines our gender, and He has given us related authority. We must tap into it and use it for His Glory. What an awesome God!

We must understand that being fashioned by God is not about what we wear on the outside, but rather what He has put within us. The characteristics and traits God incorporated into our DNA are sealed with love, peace, and grace. To rule the world, we must tap into our purpose with intention and clarity. This requires self-reflection and work. The journey that each individual takes looks different. Therefore, it is important to stay focused on your own path.

Fearfully and Wonderfully Created

As fearfully and wonderfully created women, anatomically we hold and possess the ability to carry and birth life because God gave us a womb. Our wombs hold God's promise, and it is our mission to birth it. Walking in authority is easier when we understand what we hold within. We must seek God daily to birth His promise.

Fashioned by God to Rule the World

By birthright, women possess the ability to set and or change the temperature in the room. Proverbs 14:1 explains that a wise woman builds her own house; but with her own hands a foolish one tears it down. How excellent it is that as women, we have been designed to shape the environment, atmosphere, and security of our homes and workspaces. We are fearfully and wonderfully made to shift atmospheres and reflect the peace of God. Tapping into exactly how you as a woman can consistently create what you want is key to ruling your world. Learn as much as you can about who you are and how you are created, and then move in excellence.

Acknowledging God in Creating

How can you acknowledge God in everything that you do? Thanking God in advance for what you have visualized and manifested is a wonderful way to start. Believing that God is going to give you the wisdom for how to tackle your plans and praying over them is key as well. If you plan to open a boutique and sell trailblazing fashion and trends for women, pray and praise God in advance. Before you purchase clothing or material to create looks for your clients, pray that your work is a blessing to all who come in contact with you. He will do just that and more as you acknowledge Him in everything you do. You will see God bless your finished work and draw in more clients and partnerships, because you included and acknowledged Him in every aspect.

Acknowledging God in all you do requires that you know who you are as a human and woman. Knowing who you are requires emotional and spiritual accountability. I had to realize that knowing myself changes as I gain more experience in life, as I age, and as I expand my knowledge of who God has created me to be. As a woman I learned early on that I am loving and nurturing. I desire to push as many people toward success as possible. I also had to learn as a woman that when a person is an "assignment of love," I should not make them into a partner, close friend, or even a husband. Acknowledging God in all of my desires, and learning who I am, has consistently taught me how important it is to put Him at the forefront.

Substance in Creating

Hebrews 11:1 says, "Now faith is the substance of things hoped for the evidence of things not seen." There are a few definitions of the word *substance* that I'd like to share. Meriam-Webster's Dictionary defines substance as 1. essential nature: essence, and 2. ultimate reality that underlies all outward manifestations and change. Creating a "PowHerhouse life" requires that what we desire to create has both substance and meaning, and will promote kingdom-building to the Glory of God. The substance of creating is the Spirit of God.

Remember, God's spirit moved on the water and created all that we need. Allowing the substance of the Spirit of God to move on your hands if you are a seamstress or a surgeon, or your heart when you work with people is wise. Anoint the part of your body and or mind that you will use to create and express your gift and or creation. This is imperative to achieve optimal success for your specific path. May your plan to create be filled with the substance and anointing that only is designed for you.

Hope in Creating

Hope supports faith in the process of creating. Psalm 31:24 says, "Be of good courage, and he shall strengthen your heart, all ye that hope in the Lord." Hope strengthens your passion and creative spirit at heart. A PowHerhouse creator walks, talks, and lives in a place of hope. Daily, she taps into the hope of life, promise, and love, propelling herself closer to creating her predetermined destiny. She knows that the trials of life will come. And there will be times that will cause her to bend and stretch beyond belief. She knows, however, that she must hold on to hope.

Before the divorce between my children's father and I was final, I'd almost lost all hope in God. I felt as if I had been forgotten. I had given up an excellent paying contract working for a school district in North Carolina. During the summer I started working at a private speech practice with someone I had known for many years. I was financially strapped, due to not receiving help from my children's father, and took a nearly $5,000 pay cut. I only had a small number of speech clients who were, at times, over two hours away. I remember waiting in stores for money to be wired to me, just so that I could put gas in my tank and make it back home from client visits. I truly felt like God had abandoned me.

I remember sending a message to my friend who owned the speech practice where I was working. I stated that I was not able to turn in paperwork or see clients because I did not have gas for my car. Unfortunately, she did not believe me, and thought that I was trying to take advantage of her. I prayed, *Lord please do not leave my children and I in this "barely enough" lifestyle.*

Soon, God blessed me to bring in more clients and gain employment with skilled nursing facilities as a PRN, or an as needed speech pathologist, and things began to turn around. That same year, one of my childhood friends who happened to be our neighbor, spoke with the superiors at her job about my children and I without me knowing. They adopted us for Christmas that year. It was at this point that my faith in God began to rebound. The hope that God would deliver me from such a depleted place had returned. I had to continue working hard to keep up my belief that He would sustain me through those times

Integrity in Creating

The definition of integrity is the quality of being honest and having strong moral principles. Creating a legacy, keeping your standards and core beliefs at the forefront of everything you do, requires integrity. Keeping my word on behalf of and to my children is important to me as a parent. What I have realized even more within the last few years, is the importance of maintaining the same level of integrity for myself. As women, at times we show up with integrity in business, at church, and for everyone else but we leave ourselves out.

Over the years I've often allowed life challenges and influences to distract my creative process. I second guessed myself and questioned my ability complete a project or idea. I would not keep the same level of integrity for myself, that I gave to others. Once I realized this, I shifted. When we are creating, we must keep our word and be intentional with ourselves as much as we do with other people.

Now Faith

Living and moving into a place of "now faith" is imperative when you are creating. "Now faith" is faith that is present for current and relevant life circumstances. What does your "now faith" look like? It is having the faith to believe in something you have already received or seen manifest. However, having now faith during times of adversity is a key component to creating. Now faith is for present circumstances, while faith itself will sustain you until whatever you are creating comes to fruition.

There have been many changes, highs, lows, challenges, and critical points in my life. I am so grateful that my mother named me Faith. Hearing a person call my name reminds me of my foundation and that God loves me just as I am. It is my mantra to "Live in the Now Faith!" Why? It's because now faith is the substance of things hoped for, the evidence of things not seen (Hebrews 11:1).

Lately, I have taken now faith to a new realm and applied it to my life. I say that my now faith is moving in blind faith. That means that I am believing God for the promise to create my seven-figure business with the plan and vision that He gave me. Blind faith is treating each person I meet as a connection to my business and someone who is bringing God's promise to pass. Now faith keeps me in position for daily miracles.

Fashioned by God to Rule the World
Endurance and Excellence in Creating

Merriam-Webster states that endurance means the ability to withstand hardship or adversity, the act or an instance of enduring or suffering. Wikipedia defines endurance as the ability of an organism to exert itself and remain active for a long period of time, as well as its ability to resist, withstand, recover from, and gain immunity to trauma, wounds, or fatigue.

Learning and using the definition of endurance over the years, I now have a new perspective and understanding. When I was in high school, I ran track and the coach would always say that I needed to make sure my endurance was built up so that I could make it to the end of the race. He told me to train for longer distances than the races I was competing in. So, I would do just that. I would run one mile to prepare for my shorter distance races, and I would run two miles to prepare for my mile races. When the track meets came and it was time for me to run, I would recover very quickly when I was done running.

To create the life that God predestined for you, there is going to be adversity, hardships, and trauma, however, enduring through it all means that you have the antibodies to survive and excel. Ecclesiastes 9:11 says, "I returned, and saw under the sun, that the race is not to the swift, nor the battle to the strong, neither yet bread to the wise, nor yet riches to men of understanding, nor yet favor to men of skill; but time and chance happen to them all." So, build up your endurance by studying and applying God's Word, committing to daily walking in integrity and applying faith. All of these things build your endurance and immunity for the traumas of life.

Discernment in Creating

According to Merriam-Webster, discernment is defined as the quality of being able to grasp and comprehend what is obscure. Wikipedia defines discernment as the ability to obtain sharp perceptions or to judge well in the case of judgement. In my opinion, discernment is the spiritual link between the Spirit of

God and us. I feel strongly that when we are young our discernment is strong and keen. It is with life experiences and influences that we lose our ability to trust the discernment that we were given before birth.

Being able to discern the truth in relationships, friendships, work, client needs, and our finances, we must be able to see what is appropriate and best at any given time. This does not mean that we will get it right each time. It means that we must build our relationship with God in prayer, learning His Word and ways to apply specifically to our lives. Building a strong spirit of discernment does not happen at once, it is built over a lifetime.

The process of being *Fashioned by God to Rule the World* is, without a doubt, different for each person. It is our responsibility to follow the path and journey that is created specifically for each one of us. Each one may look and feel different, but ultimately the goal is to live with the love and guidance of our Creator for His Glory. By allowing God to be at the forefront of each decision, acknowledging Him, walking in faith, love, endurance and excellence, we are sure to win at life and be all that we are fashioned to be.

All of the sexual abuse, financial challenges, trauma, divorce, feelings of being unloved, and self-doubt that I have endured throughout my life, is a part of the journey that I had to endure to find my path to rule in this world. My world was fashioned before I was conceived, and despite all that I've gone through I am convinced that it has all worked out just as planned.

Journal

Fashioned by God to Rule the World

Journal

Fashioned by God to Rule the World

Chapter 2
The PowHER of Light in Innovation

Erica Holmes, MSCPE

Erica's HERstory

My name is Erica, and I was born in November 1981 in Joliet, IL. I am the loving mother of three beautiful children: Simuel 21, Jonathan 19, and Kira Lynn 13. Growing up in the Lockport/ Joliet area had its challenges, but my family members looked out for each other. My grandparents played a huge part in my growing up; they took care of my siblings and I while my mother wasn't there. I experienced difficult aspects of life early on, including molestation, rape and an understanding of the "gang life." The one thing that I truly appreciate is my spiritual upbringing. I grew up in church and as a teenager I transitioned into Greater Bibleway Apostolic Temple. This laid the groundwork of what was to come for me.

I have many skills and to be honest, I was unsure of who or what I wanted to be. I went to Fairmont School in Lockport, IL, and went on to Lockport East High School. Later I transitioned to Joliet Central High School, where I had to drop out to take care of my siblings. I graduated from the Joliet Jr. College GED program and from there I pursed a nursing degree. I became a certified nursing assistant, and then went to on to

Northwestern University to earn a bachelor's degree in biochemistry and computer science.

Finally, I attended Old Dominion University for a master's in computer engineering and programming. I've worked for Fortune 100 companies such as Apple, Blackwater, and Amazon. I'm now a serial entrepreneur with a multitude of businesses in which I invest my time, energy and heart. I am the CEO of a technology company that brings digital formation to any organization and seeks to achieve higher returns for government contracts, investors, board members and market partners through traditional and alternative markets, both foreign and domestic. This business is located primarily in northern Illinois and is growing.

I am also known as "Ms. Community" because of all of the work that I have invested in the local neighborhoods since 2012. Currently I serve as the executive director of the Harvey Brooks Foundation, which empowers youth and provides human services to the community. I sit on numerous boards for notable organizations throughout Will County, IL. I am a member of the National Hook-up of Black Women, Joliet Chapter, and I serve as the community partnership liaison for different neighborhoods. I have won several awards including businesswoman of the year, the Top 40 Under 40 Women in Technology, and a prestigious community award named after the late Dr. Isaac Singleton.

I love to read, travel, spend time with my family, find new places to dine, and build relationships. I am thankful to everyone who has had a hand in making me the person that I am today, with a special shout out to a woman that God placed in my life, Roberta Lynn Franklin. She has been like a mom to me, and a grandmother to my children. I give God all of the credit for the vision that He has placed inside of me to advance His kingdom.

Chapter 2
The PowHER of Light in Innovation

And GOD said. "Let there be light," and there was light. God saw the light was good: and he separated the light from the darkness. And GOD called the light "day" and the darkness he called "night." And there was evening and there was morning—the first day.

— Genesis 1:3-5 NIV

This passage is "powHerful" in relation to what God did in the beginning of time. He is a God of completion; He always completes His work. Understanding what God finished in the beginning, and how He finished it on the first day of creation, can enlighten us on our journeys to understanding the light that we carry. Let me share a story to help illustrate this.

In a small Midwestern town, a young girl who was full of light, was dealt a rough hand. We can call this darkness. The girl was molested by her uncle and left for dead by her teen mother, who later went to prison. God was always with the girl from the very beginning. He placed people in her life to help her see what He'd placed deep inside of her.

Despite the darkness surrounding this young girl she was able to become a beacon of light and help her grandparents raise her siblings. She was a help to anyone who had the opportunity to interact with her. This is not to say that the girl was perfect; she had moments of acting out and trying to rebel. But every time, before she could go too far, something kept tugging at her, causing her to stop. It would even wake her out of her sleep.

She started asking questions at church, in Bible study and Sunday school. More and more this young girl realized what was happening. She began to notice the powHer of the light inside of her, which she later learned was the Holy Spirit. This Spirit would allow her to grow up and become the powHer of light in innovation, that God designed her to be. The young girl would experience this powHer of light by understanding the meaning of *her* light. Similarly, we all carry light that we are given by God. We have to understand what it is in order to apply it.

This is an exciting period of time to know that the light you possess will make a difference. You have to believe that you are a powHerful light that the world needs to see. It is possible. Throughout this chapter you will see how the young girl I've been talking about has grown and come to understand her own light. By reading about her experience, I hope that you can see yourself more clearly.

The meaning of *PowHer* is understanding the power that lies within you. And just like we stated with the young girl it's the God within that guides you. Genesis 1:3 says, "And God said, let there be light: and there was light." Just like the light exists, so do you. There are a couple of ways to relate to the light— naturally and supernaturally. However, you never want to be an artificial light—that will be addressed later in this chapter.

Natural light is the light from the sun, also known as daylight according to Merriam-Webster's Dictionary. Natural light improves your productivity and focus, and as a woman of God this is needed daily. The benefits of natural light are reflected in the way that we feel. It doesn't just apply to our physical wellbeing, but also to our psychological health and moods. A lack of daylight can make us feel down, depressed and anxious. With natural light, making sure we get outside, and exposing ourselves to enough sunlight is crucial to our wellbeing. But this is only one part of ensuring we reap all of the benefits that natural light has to offer. An example of how natural light can be essential for us is proven by its provision of vitamin D, an essential building block for our bodies.

God was truly dynamic and strategic in His original design. Do you see how important it is to understand natural light? How important it is to recognize the natural light in our natural state as women? I ask these questions as a way to make you think about light in a different way, as a foundation, so that you can truly understand God's plan for you.

Now, let's talk about the supernatural light, which is God's Son, Jesus Christ. In John 8:12 (NIV), when Jesus spoke again to the people, He said, "I am the LIGHT of the world. Whoever follows me will never walk in darkness but will have the LIGHT of life. Sis, understand that the light that dwells within you has provided you resources and energy beyond what natural light can do. The light within actually gave you life! Can you see how amazing God is? He established light on the first day, in the beginning, so that you can always have life. Be encouraged to know that the powHer is found in the light. Do you know what's deep inside of you? Do you understand the supernatural light that guides you?

The young girl that we spoke about earlier was able to see her supernatural light through the Word of God. She saw how God was with her the entire time. Just like He said in Joshua 1:9 (NIV), "Have I not commanded you? Be strong and courageous. Do not be afraid; do not be discouraged, for the Lord your GOD will be with you wherever you go." Let the light within you be the source to help and guide you like the young girl. You see, she will grow into a woman that God will use to get the glory. And He can use her because of the faith she had in the supernatural light—the Holy Spirit.

Now, that I have laid the foundation regarding natural and supernatural light, let's get into understanding the powHer of the light that you as a woman possess. Remember, God was intentional and strategic when He formed you. I know you are wondering how I know that. Well, let's talk about it by looking at how you were designed. God was innovative before innovation was a "thing".

> *Genesis 2:21-23 (NIV) says, "So the Lord God caused the man to fall into a deep sleep; and while he was sleeping, he took one of the man's ribs and then closed up the place with flesh. Then the Lord God made a woman from the rib, he had taken out of the man, and he brought her to the man. The man said, "This is now bone of my bones and flesh of my*

flesh; she shall be called 'woman,' for she was taken out of man."

You have been created for greatness and the powHer you possess is within you. Look at how Eve was able to convince Adam to eat even though it was wrong. She was able to get him to do something that God had forbidden him to do. That's deep. Understanding the true powHer of what we as women carry, we have to be able to utilize it in a positive and constructive way. God has to get the glory out of what we do. Let's look at how the young girl was able to recognize this in her life.

Early on, the young girl realized she possessed the attribute of influence. She was able to convince others that the way to God—through Jesus—was the only way. In 1992, the young girl experienced a life-changing event at an amusement park. She was just in the fourth grade and was injured. The teachers and other students were horrified. But the young girl showed how the light inside of her was so powHerful that it made everyone pay attention to the fact she was stable. After the injury, she prayed to God and wasn't ashamed about what had happened. The teacher and the doctor prayed with her. Having faith to know that God was going to work it out was key. What the young girl did without realizing it was to express confidence in her prayer. She knew that God could turn her situation around.

That's what we all need to do; get into a place of being confident and aware of who God designed us to be. Did you know that you are the Proverbs 31 woman that God describes?

> *Proverbs 31 says, "A wife of noble character who can find? She is worth more far more than rubies. Her husband has full confidence in her and lacks nothing of value. She brings him good, not harm, all the days of her life. She selects wool and flax and works with eager hands. She is like the merchant ships, bringing her food from afar. She gets up while it is still night; she provides food for her family and portions for her female servants. She considers a field and buys it; out of her earnings she plants a vineyard. She sets about her work*

vigorously; her arms are strong for her tasks. She sees that her trading is profitable, and her lamp does not go out at night."

The scripture goes on from there and you can read it for yourself. But my goodness, it is truly talking about all women—about you. I know some who are reading this will say I am not a wife. While that may be true, you are still the woman this scripture references.

To know who you are, you have to look at the amazing format that has been established for you. If anything, you should strive to be this Proverbs 31 woman. Trust that the ability is within you. Remember the light. Yes, it is there! The scripture speaks to how we as women are viewed and desired. That's why it is important to know who you are; you don't want to be pulled into darkness.

I mentioned earlier that I would discuss darkness further, and what it sometimes can look like in our world. We are not going to be perfect all of the time, or even be the light that we need to be for ourselves. Eve brought darkness to God's creation when she was deceived by the serpent. The darkness mentioned in Genesis 1:3-5 was showing how the entire day was made. There had to be separation between day and night. However, darkness has a symbolic meaning that we can't ignore. Understanding darkness will help you understand how important it is to be the light.

Supernaturally, we know the light is God working within us; with the same token we know that the devil is the prince of darkness. Even in the book of Revelation, darkness indicates that the end of the world is forthcoming. Darkness also can be a symbol of bad judgement, misfortune, and ignorance. Realize that although you may have dark moments, you are not the darkness. John 1:4-5 (NIV) says, "In him (God) was life, and that life was the light of mankind. The light shines in the darkness, and the darkness has not overcome it."

That's it! Darkness can't overpower your powHerful light. Remember, the young girl? She experienced sexual abuse from someone who was close to her. This was darkness that plagued her life. Her innocence and purity were taken away. She was violated and couldn't change what happened. It caused her to grow up faster. But through it all, God was still with her. The light that shone through her would cause the darkness to go away.

In 1988, that darkness went away and would never return because her perpetrator was killed. She was safe from that darkness. While she would never wish death on anyone, her prayers were answered, and now she has been able to grow and heal from that betrayal and hurt. According to 2 Timothy 4:18, the Lord will rescue us from every evil attack and will bring us safely to his heavenly kingdom. To him be glory for ever and ever. Amen.

How many women do you know have similar stories? That is why as women we are unique; we were designed to be conquerors, overcomers. God made us so that we would rule the world with the light that lies within us.

Now it is time to apply the powHer of light in an innovative way. The foundation has been laid for you to understand the light and its powHer. Then the darkness, though it follows the light to complete a full day, is does not represent who we are. It's not who we are, however, we now have a better understanding of how to combat it. Being the light is key to make sure God gets the glory. In Matthew 5:14-16 (NIV), Jesus says, "You are the Light of the world. A town built on a hill cannot be hidden. Neither do people light a lamp and put it under a bowl. Instead, they put it on its stand, and it gives light to everyone in the house. In the same way, let your light shine before others, that they may see your good deeds and glorify your Father in heaven."

This is how we are to apply the light! We have to implement the innovation that Jesus has set forth; this means to continue with the success of being the light. Titus 2:3-5 says, "Likewise, teach the older women to be reverent in the way they live, not to be slanderers or addicted to much wine, but to teach what is good. Then they can urge the younger women to love their husbands and children, to be self-controlled and pure, to be busy at home, to be kind, and to be subject to their husbands, so that no one will malign (slander) the word of GOD."

Today, the young girl is all grown up, and she is similar to Deborah in the book of Judges. She leads her community in the same way, where God gets the Glory, and she has been innovative in her approach. I encourage you to read Judges 4:1-24 (NIV), which lays out for us who Deborah was and how she innovated in her role as a prophet and judge. We see how Deborah became the light that people needed to be rescued and God was with her the entire time. Even more importantly, you will notice that others' lights also were used to get the job done. Be the light and use it for the betterment of the kingdom of GOD.

You have the foundation and the basis to understand the light that is within you is powHerful. As women, we possess something that is so needed. As a grown woman, the young girl is now a beacon of light for others. She inspires and motivates others to see the powHer that was within her from the beginning.

You should now understand the purpose and intention of the light, and despite life experiences you don't ever have to become the darkness. You can have the confidence and the know how to move forward, apply the powHer of light to innovate, starting today. How can I know this for sure? Because I am the young girl.

Fashioned by God to Rule the World

Journal

Journal

Fashioned by God to Rule the World

Chapter 3
The Seasons of a Woman's Life

Barbara Ellzey

Barbara's HERstory

Barbara A. Ellzey was ordained under the P.A.W. Inc. and serves as an evangelist under the Pastorate of Bishop Horace E. Smith, M.D., at the Apostolic Faith Church in Chicago, IL. She has served as a Sunday school teacher, retreat and conference coordinator, workshop presenter for women's ministries, advisory board committee member to the Ministerial Alliance, and in roles for various other ministries.

For eight years she served as the lay director of AFC Prayer Ministries, Faith Works Broadcast Prayer Ministries and chaplain of Kenwood Nursing Home. Evangelist Ellzey ministers through the Word of God with passion, transparency and a love for God's people. A lover of prayer, she's held prayer meetings in downtown Chicago or eleven years and led many souls to Christ. For more than twelve years, Barbara's passion and love for her community have been exhibited by her spiritual guidance, and creativity through her philanthropy and REACH program.

In 2009, Barbara founded Reach the Leadership Program for Girls in loving memory of her mother, Thelma Lee Redmond, who succumbed to cancer a few years prior. The purpose of this program is to empower girls to make positive and informed life decisions by providing year-round mentoring, enriching activities, training programs, and informative workshops. The Reach Leadership Program for Girls builds self-esteem, promotes abstinence and bullying prevention, offers modules for healthy peer relationships, college preparation, anger management, and best practices for conflict resolution. To further impact their outlook on careers, REACH will teach aviation through a new collaboration. This endeavor will positively broaden the young ladies' ambitions in career options. All of this culminates with Barbara's dedication to fundraising and networking with businesses in her community via efforts such as her annual Big Hats Brunch.

Beyond REACH, her passion for community outreach includes acts of philanthropy in partnering with her local women's shelter and homeless outreach initiatives. Examples include coat drives, sponsoring 500 purses filled with hygiene products, and Christmas care packages for those in need. In addition, yearly Barbara raises funds to purchase trunks for first-time college students.

Barbara has received numerous awards including the Chicago Defender Women of Excellence, Chicago Skyy WNBA Redefining Leadership Award, Chicago Bulls I AM WOMAN OF IMPACT 2020 Award, and the Chicago Commissioner Lowry 2021 Unsung Heroine Award.

Chapter 3
The Seasons of a Woman's Life

And God said, let there be lights in the firmament of the heaven to divide the day from the night; and let them be for signs, and for seasons, and for days, and years.

—Genesis 1:14

I think of women as beautiful flowers, arrayed in breathtaking colors with different scents to tantalize the senses. Each flower is designated to bloom at its appointed time after the growth cycle. While some flower growth cycles may be longer or shorter, the anticipation of the end result is always delightful. God made so many beautiful things on earth, so many masterpieces. But underneath all of these wonderful creations… was dirt.

When God created the heavens and the earth there was no form; void and darkness was upon the face of the deep. It wasn't until the Creator God said, let there be heaven and its populaces, and earth as we know it came into existence. It wasn't until God said, "Let us make man in our image, after our likeness: and let them have dominion!" that the Bible said the Lord God formed man of the dust of the ground and breathed into his nostrils the breath of life; and man became a living soul.

I've heard preachers say the "woman" was personified in the man but hadn't been called forth yet. But oh, when He called us forth the game changed. With exquisiteness, beauty, gentleness, and wisdom, the scent of a woman permeated the garden. Time stood still, the flowers leaned in, the birds stopped singing, and all of creation took notice. With the emergence of woman, it was God's finest hour. As the millennials would say, "God did that!"

Throughout the Bible women have had a presence. According to Wikipedia, women in the Bible are victors and victims, women who change the course of historical events, and women who are powerless to affect their own destinies. The majority of them are unnamed, with women making up less than ten percent of all named people in the Bible. Women are not generally in the forefront of public life in the Bible, and women who are named are usually prominent for other than ordinary reasons.

For example, they are often involved in the overturning of human power structures in a common biblical literary device called "reversal." Abigail and Esther, and Jael, who drove a tent peg into the enemy commander's temple while he slept, are examples of women who turned the tables on men with power.

The founding matriarchs are mentioned by name, as are some prophetesses, judges, heroines, and queens, while the common or lower stationed woman is largely, though not completely, unseen. The slave Hagar's story is told, and the prostitute Rahab's story is also told, among a few others.

The New Testament refers to a number of women in Jesus' inner circle, and He is generally seen by scholars as dealing with women, with respect. The New Testament names women in positions of leadership in the early church as well. And there are controversies within the contemporary Christian church concerning women. For example, Mary Magdalene's role as a leader is disputed. Sexuality has played a major role in these issues which have impacted, and continue to impact, how the modern Christian church sees the role of women. These changing views of women in the Bible are reflected in art and culture.

As little girls, we are imitators of our mothers' qualities. We mimic their behavior, strutting around the house with their high heels on, playing with their wigs, jewelry and makeup, pretending to be someone we're clearly not, yet. As we move through the stages and development of life, we encounter people, places and things that begin to take part in shaping who we are becoming. As a young girl, I was a relentless dreamer, envisioning my future to be bright and full of laughter. I imagined that I'd live in a beautiful home and have many daughters. God changed that dream and gave me laughter and a warm home, with two lovely daughters and an incredible son.

As time moves forward, and one season after another escorts us down the winding roads of life each season prepares us for the next. I particularly enjoy the fall; it gives us the opportunity to exhale and breathe in new oxygen. Spiritually speaking, fall represents the harvest time of year. It's a time for growth, expansion, beginning anew, relaxing with a soothing cup of tea and reevaluating your steps from the previous nine months.

Fall is a perfect time to think about the many goals and plans you wrote down at the beginning of the year. It gives you a chance to look at all you desired to accomplish, how these things were to be implemented, who would benefit from them, and whether or not there would there be any indelible imprints made along the way. This new spiritual season is filled with changes, challenges and triumphs that need your eager participation and obedience as God elevates you to a place you've never been before.

While new seasons bring feelings of excitement, they also usher in uncertainty and a hopeful expectation that God is up to something and will do great and new things. New seasons can make you uncomfortable, where you will no longer fit the pond that you have grown accustomed to. Discomfort will increasingly grow as you prolong the stay in your familiar place. To all who are facing a new season in life, whether it includes marriage, divorce, gaining or losing the ideal job, parenting, or death of a loved one, the Bible assures us to trust in the Lord always.

In Isaiah 40:28-31 the scriptures remind us that, the Lord the Everlasting God, the Creator of all the earth, He will not grow tired or weary. It reminds us that God's unfailing love is with us. As Lamentations 3:22-33 says, it is of the Lord's mercies that we are not consumed, because his compassions fail not. They are new every morning: great is thy faithfulness! Daniel 2:21 tells us that He changes the times and seasons. He removes kings and sets up kings; He gives wisdom to the wise and knowledge to those who have understanding. Jeremiah 29:11 contains a precious promise for all Christians the world over. In this verse, Jeremiah affirms that God is in control and, moreover, He has good things in store: "For I know the plans I have for you, declares the LORD, plans for good and not of evil to give you a future and a hope."

Jeremiah 29:11 is not a promise to immediately rescue us from hardship or suffering, but rather it is a promise that God has a plan for our lives. Regardless of our current situation, He can work through it to prosper and give us a hope. From this scripture we can know that change is coming but so is character development, the purging of old ways, and travailing.

Recently, I read an interesting social media post, "A shark in a fish tank will grow up to eight inches long, but in the ocean, it will grow to eight feet or more. The shark will never outgrow its environment. The same is true about you. Many times, we're surrounded by small-thinking people, so we don't grow. When God nudges us into a new season, He magnifies those things within you that you cannot bring along. The removal of such things will make you uncomfortable. You will no longer fit, and the discomfort will increasingly grow as you prolong change to stay attached to the familiar. Oftentimes, with growth it is your heart that God is seeking after.

The Bible uses the heart primarily to refer to the ruling center of the whole person, the spring of all desires, the home of the personal life. The heart, according to the Bible, is the part of the Christian's spiritual makeup. It is the place where emotions and desires begin; that which drives the will of man towards action.

Jeremiah 17:9 describes the heart as being deceitful above all things, and desperately wicked who can know it? The prophet goes on to say that I the Lord search the heart, I try the reins, even to give man according to his ways, and according to the fruit of his doings.

Proverbs 4:23 says to keep thy heart with all diligence for out of it are the issues of life.

In Psalm 51:10, David says, create in me a clean heart, O God and renew a right spirit within me.

First Samuel 16:7 says, But the Lord said unto Samuel, look not on his countenance, or on the height of his stature; because I have refused him: for the Lord seeth not as man seeth; for man looketh on the outward appearance, but the Lord looketh on the heart.

Ezekial 36:26 goes on to say a new heart also will I give you, and a new spirit will I put within you: and I will take away the stony heart out of your flesh, and I will give you an heart of flesh.

Through His Word, God is saying if you want to successfully change the season of your life and walk in the purpose that He has designed for you, He must be allowed to enter the depths of your heart. You must give Him access to the dark places to eliminate, do away with, get rid of, and destroy every seed that wasn't planted by Him.

In Matthew 15:13 Jesus said, every plant, which my heavenly Father hath not planted, shall be rooted up. The past is the past, which means it must not be a leading factor in your life if you are to embrace your new season, glory to God! Your past could very well be a vehicle to catapult you into your future! In Philippians 3:13-14 Paul wrote, "Forgetting those things which are behind and reaching forward to those things ahead. I press towards the mark of the high calling of God in Jesus Christ."

Each child of God designed after His image has a high calling and an even higher purpose to affect the world. This is especially the case for women today. No one can deny that we are in the "seasons of a woman's life." Women are making powerful moves, with numerous articles written in *Forbes* and *Business Insider* about our efforts in fighting the pandemic to reengineering American politics. Influential women are making history, with some even achieving success later in life!

From the boardroom, to Hollywood, to the floor of the House of Representatives, women today are making their presence known. Movements such as "Me Too" and "Time's Up" are maintaining momentum, and more women are involved in politics than ever before. We all witnessed history on January 20, 2021 when Senator Kamala Harris was sworn in as the first female and first Black and South Asian vice president of the United States. After being confirmed as vice president-elect in 2020, Kamala Harris addressed the nation from Wilmington, Delaware, saying, "While I may be the first woman in this office, I will not be the last, because every little girl watching tonight sees that this is a country of possibilities." Along with Vice President Harris, President Joe Biden nominated twelve women to Cabinet positions, including eight women of color. Additionally, history was made as some departments had never been headed by a female or a particular race.

Women shined in politics, and film wasn't far behind. Over the last twelve months, according to an annual gender study, a record number of female directors headed major Hollywood films. The annual Celluloid Ceiling report by San Diego State University found that women accounted for sixteen percent of directors working on the 100 highest grossing films in 2020.

The year 2020 was unprecedented on many fronts, and women's sports were also part of that. Female athletes changed sports history. We all cheered for the accomplishments of Serena Williams; she's won twenty-three Grand Slam Singles titles in her twenty-five-year career, the most won by any man or woman in the open era.

Many of us have cheered for the accomplishments of Oprah, Michelle Obama, Kamala Harris, Serena Williams, Shonda Rhimes, Ava DuVernay, Issa Rae, inauguration day poet, Amanda Gorman, famous women singers, ordinary mothers on the front lines making a difference in their local communities, and so many other successful women.

But I'd like to pause to ask a question: what has God spoken to you about your season to affect the world? What dreams have you placed on the shelf, and ultimately what's stopping you from beginning to pursue and present them to the world? Dreams are part of your life, yet it can sometimes feel impossible to make them real. You might know what to do and even how do it, but taking action requires courage. You need to have the ability to withstand fear, humiliation, and discomfort.

As children, we innocently dream and talk of the future, and if those dreams are not nurtured with love but are met with negativity, we become conditioned to avoid unpleasant feelings. Nothing stirs those feelings like someone believing in you and encouraging you to take the necessary risks.

Dreams demand taking a leap of faith, focusing on strategies, conditioning your mind to deal with 'haters' and letting go of people's opinions that hold no value! I often share and believe that before people's opinions, God has a purpose for your life.

The need for approval has been ingrained in us since childhood. However, tying your worth to what other people think sets you up for disappointment by forgoing what matters most to you, and doing things you believe will make them happy. When you let go of the need to please others, you're free to be yourself. Otherwise, you're only trying to get people to like you by pretending to be someone else.

In reality, even if they approve of your actions, it's not the real you that they like. Discontent is being disconnected from your authentic self. Pursuing and achieving your dreams takes courage and growth as you strive to make the dream a reality and may I say, taking the dream or vision from within your mind and writing it on paper is half the battle to achieving your goal.

The "Seasons of a Woman's Life" bring joy and pain, changes, transformation, and times of isolation. When I think of transformation, the metamorphosis of the butterfly is a great example. When I see a beautifully colored butterfly, I've rarely given thought to the wrenching process that the caterpillar had to endure. Upon researching the caterpillar's process, I found an article written by *National Geographic* that states when the caterpillar is ready to transform, it "releases enzymes that break down many of its tissues into proteins."

In the chrysalis, the hard shell in which the caterpillar is encased, some organs stay intact, but others get broken into pieces that look like building blocks ready to be re-purposed as muscle, wing structure and color. Also, in the transformation, the chrysalis drastically reduces its gut material and increases its breathing tubes and mechanisms. The chrysalis becomes a glorious network, with the body of the butterfly becoming nearly lighter than air.

The last week of December 2020, I waited with bated breath in anticipation for the year to close. That last Tuesday morning, I wept in prayer before God and said, "Lord if you allow me to cross over to 2021, I'm going to run for you like never before." God spoke back to me and said *fix this*. I immediately knew what "this" was. Humbly, I submitted, and I did what He told me to do.

On New Year's Day, I exhaled and decided to put my heart on the altar so that the light of God could search the dark places and the fire of God would burn up everything that wasn't like Him. Placing my heart on the altar and relying on God's guidance has led me from one open door to another; and the journey continues!

I believe we each have a divine call to allow transformation to take place. We are called to courageously step up and say, "I'm ready to become who and what I am meant to be." This requires faith and it requires the desire to transform. If you want to become something new, you first need to know who and what you already are. Take time to search within and see the truth of who you are, and the truth of who you desire to be. Be honest with yourself about your weaknesses and strengths, and what might be blocking you from getting to where you want to be.

Butterflies don't just magically pop out of caterpillars. It takes work to build the cocoon of transformation, and time to enter in and remain until the butterfly is ready to emerge. Take your time setting goals, understanding the process of change, and working on the change you desire. Work on your talents. Practice. Seek new learning opportunities and share what you have to offer in small doses. Let yourself be in the "season" of life you are in.

As you build and enter your chrysalis give yourself space to prepare. While in the chrysalis don't overstay. You are not meant to remain in the cocoon of transformation forever. Have faith. Believe in yourself and if you lack self-confidence, work on it. Surround yourself with people that desire the best for you, people who want to see you excel, who will help push you to overcome your fears and reluctance. Get around people who will celebrate you.

Believe in the process that God has established for you to emerge as a beautiful design, on display for the world to see. Women as you are moving through seasons of life, change gracefully, change beautifully, and change confidently. Grow with other women. Compliment and collaborate with them. Don't compete.

I am a proud mother to my three young adults, and nothing brings me more joy than having conversations with each of them. My two daughters are married, and I call them just to hear the latest stories of their marriages. I holler with laughter while they share each funny story. When they say "mom don't laugh" I holler even louder.

The "Seasons of a Woman's Life" bring authentic living, doing what's right and being true to who you really are with appreciation for the good and the bad. Women of purpose, leading unapologetically, embracing your true self.

Queen, remember that you are beautiful and intelligent. You have to keep your promises to yourself and not be afraid. You are dynamic, you are a force to be reckoned with. Girl you rock!

Journal

Journal

Fashioned by God to Rule the World

Chapter 4
RuleHERship for Women

Sheriolyn Curry, MDiv, CSA

Sheriolyn's HERstory

Sheriolyn M. Curry is inspirational. She is a CEO, a preacher, teacher, church planter, entrepreneur and life coach who loves watching lives transform. Her mission is to serve, empower others to use their God-given gifts, and to advance the kingdom of God. As a student of all things joyful, she goes by the social persona of "Dr. Joy."

In her early twenties, God called Sheriolyn to ministry. After a series of life events, including having a recurring dream over a twenty-year period, in 2003 she accepted the call. She was ordained an itinerant deacon in 2005 under Bishop John R. Bryant, and an itinerant elder in 2008 under Bishop T. Larry Kirkland. Sheriolyn earned a Master of Divinity from Fuller Theological Seminary in 2008.

Rev. Curry has held many leadership roles in the church, including youth minister, member of the Board of Trustees,

Fashioned by God to Rule the World

finance committee, Board of Examiners and the Desert Mountain Conference Coordinator of Women in Ministry. Rev. Curry is the founding pastor of Mt. Moriah Community AME Church in Maricopa, AZ, and the former pastor of Greater Bethel AME Church in Phoenix, AZ. She currently serves as the presiding elder of the Rocky Mountain District in the Desert Mountain Conference, 5th Episcopal District, of the African Methodist Episcopal Church.

Since 2002, she has been the CEO and owner of several Comfort Keepers franchise offices, headquartered in Chandler, AZ. As a leading provider of non-medical home care services for senior adults, they are not only a first-thought provider for these types of services, but also educate and support families caring for loved ones in long-term care situations.

Sheriolyn has proven community leadership, having served on numerous boards and organizations, including Seeking Doors, Inc., Junior Achievement, and the African American Advisory Council for Congressional District 7 under Congressman Ruben Gallego. She is a charter member of the National Coalition of 100 Black Women Phoenix Metropolitan Chapter (2015); and a proud forty-four-year member of Alpha Kappa Alpha Sorority, Inc. She's received numerous leadership awards including the Positively Powerful Woman Award for Spiritual Leadership in 2012, and the NAACP 2016 Image Award for Religion, the Global Women's Summit Award for Leadership and the Desert Mountain Conference YPD Pastor of the Year.

Rev. Curry has an amazingly diverse, perfectly imperfect family. She has two daughters, four grandsons, and a host of bonus daughters and grandchildren. Siblings, nieces and nephews, cousins and an aunt round out her familial circle. In her free time, she loves to write, complete jigsaw puzzles and spend time with her grandchildren.

Her favorite scripture is Ephesians 3:20-21, "Now to him who is able to do far more abundantly than all that we ask, or think, according to the power at work within us, to him be glory in the church and in Christ Jesus throughout all generations, forever and ever."

Chapter 4
RuleHERship for Women

Then God said, "Let us make humankind in our image, in our likeness; so they may rule over the fish of the sea, and the birds in the sky, and over the livestock and over all the wild animals, and over all the creatures that move along the ground." So God created humankind in his own image, in the image of God he created them; male and female he created them. God blessed them and said to them, "Be fruitful and increase in number; fill the earth and subdue it. Rule over the sea and the birds in the sky and over every living creature that moves on the ground. God saw all that he had made, and it was very good. And there was evening, and there was morning – the sixth day.

—Genesis 1:26-28, 31

Introduction

Thank you for taking the time to read this book, and welcome to chapter four. This chapter is a reflection of woman's ruleHERship assignment, found in Genesis 1:26-31, as well as my own journey in leadership. For the purposes of our time together, I will use the verbs "to rule" and "to lead," as well as the offices of "rulership" and "leadership" interchangeably.

The intention for this chapter is straightforward—to empower women, and men, to embrace the leadership shift with optimism, create space for "additions" to the guard, and to reframe what leading in the changed world we now live in should look like, as it was designed to be from the beginning. Woven throughout are my threefold objectives for the reader:

> 1) Empower women who were told that they could never be leaders, were never supposed to lead, or didn't have leadership characteristics to embrace their God-given assignment and authority to do so,

2) Support women, and men, in shifting their viewpoint of women as leaders and co-leaders. This shift is necessary due to errant teachings and misinformation, much of which were a form of oppression and suppression, and

3) Free women who have bought into the misguided thought that only men should, or could, rule. Oftentimes they don't even remember where they developed this thinking, particularly as it relates to women leading men in the church, not understanding that it is generational teaching. When we don't question, or at least explore alternatives using evidenced based thought, it can lead to a single way of thinking and a proliferation of errant and unintentional behaviors. It's the thinking of this third group that is most dangerous as it pits women against women and undermines God's entire design for the rule of the world, which is to be done in partnership.

As you read this chapter, I encourage you to do so with an open mind, seeking truth, and withholding judgment. If you do this, I am certain that your personal call to action will be clear. At the very least, I pray that it is a thought-provoking read, worthy of your sharing it with someone for whom you care.

In the Beginning...Fashioned by God

In Genesis 1:1 we read that in the beginning, there was chaos. The precise nature of this chaos is hard to define, but what we are sure of from reading the text, is that there was this great expanse, and it was without form and it was empty, and it was dark. We have come to understand chaos to mean complete disorder and confusion, but there is no suggestion that this expanse was a result of some cosmic blow up that left everything in shambles. Quite the contrary, it is simply described as formless, empty and dark. There was no order, there was no shape, no structure, purpose or direction. The condition or state of the universe reflected "the face of the deep," meaning it was uninhabitable and not capable of sustaining life.

Then God began the creative process. We read in Genesis 1:3-25 that it pleased God to spend six days creating, placing, organizing, and balancing the universe. On God's command, order was brought forth out of the chaos, and everything that was created was given an assignment, specific instructions as to its function in the universe. Everything had its purpose, and was part of the universal masterpiece, hand painted by God. And everything, I do mean everything, God determined was either good or very good. Let that sink in for a moment.

Fashioned as Leaders to Rule…The Assignments

God created humankind in his own image, in the image of God he created them; male and female he created them. God blessed them and said to them, "Be fruitful and increase in number; fill the earth and subdue it. Rule over the sea and the birds in the sky and over every living creature that moves on the ground."

—Genesis 1:27-28 (NIV)

In verse 27, when God fashioned male and female in His image, they were created in a unique way, in a privileged position, and for a different purpose than the earlier created things. In all the other created order, God said, "Let there be…" and it was. When the time came for the creation of human beings, something unique happened. God went into counsel with Himself, as evidenced by Him saying, "Let us…," as if the created being was so special that a collaborative discussion and decision was warranted. The Bible tells us in Psalm 139:14 that we are fearfully and wonderfully made. The Contemporary English Version puts it like this: "and I praise you because of the wonderful way you created me. Everything you do is marvelous! Of this I have no doubt."

Fashioned by God to Rule the World

God said, let us make humankind in our image. This would suggest that the community of the Godhead, the trinity—God the Father, God the Son and God the Holy Spirit—is one, and we were made in their image. This also totally set us apart from any other created being as none of creation prior to humankind was created in the image of God. This has consequences regarding our relationship with each other and how we live out this earthly walk.

This is significant. First of all, it means that every human being resembles the Creator in some way. We are all important, special, worthy and God-filled. This also means that we should recognize the Creator in every other human being, regardless of their gender, color, ethnicity, creed, etc. Finally, we can conclude without reservation that all lives matter to God. There is no one lesser than, or greater than another.

To understand this fact is to understand that God plays no favorites. We are all precious in His sight. Acts 10:23-48 (MSG) records the story of Peter being summoned to the home of Cornelius, a non-Jew, so he could hear the good news that Peter was preaching. The Bible tells us that Peter was so excited and said, "It's God's own truth, nothing could be plainer: God plays no favorites! It makes no difference who you are or where you're from—if you want God and are ready to do as he says, the door is open," (Acts 10:34). Understanding this also helps us with the command to love our neighbors as ourselves. All humans were made in the image of God.

In Genesis 1:38, the human beings were blessed by God, and given their assignments. Hear me on this, they both were given the same instructions. Male and female, equally. The first was to be fruitful and multiply, to fill the earth. That speaks to legacy. The second instruction was to rule over creation and to subdue the earth.

Let me stop here and remind us of God's original intent for ruling. It was to keep order. It was intended to keep the order of the good and very good that God had so meticulously created, the design so intricately planned, the faith so confidently placed in humans to rule, tend to and take care of the created things. In case you forgot what those were, read chapter 1 verses 1-25. It was the birds of the air, the fish in the sea and the land creatures. All of creation prior to the creation of human beings. How hard was that? What could go wrong? Well, apparently a lot, and it begins with understanding the "rule," how it was to be done and by whom.

Here's what's key. Man was never given authority to dominate woman, and neither woman the man. There is no reading of this text where it can be construed to mean that we rule over each other. We each bear the image of God, and as such, His nature. But each were given the task of ruling, which is to serve. Women were given the *same* instructions, at the *same* time, for co-rulership, and with it all of the responsibility, gifting, graces and authority to do so. There was no delineation of gender roles in who would do the ruling. None. In essence, it can absolutely be concluded, without contradiction or rebuttal, that women were fashioned by God to rule the world.

But that's not what we have been taught. Women weren't taught that in the home, in school or in church. It was not instilled in us that we could be leaders over the world! Women were taught that they could be secretaries, teachers and homemakers and wives and mothers, all of those nurturing kinds of roles, using skills which we naturally bring to the table. And, Lord knows, these are admirable, honorable, and much needed traits. However, in all roles, there are opportunities for rulership. And creation will only thrive, if it's done decently and in order.

Historically, there are a few women of exception who don't fit this generalization. They are the trailblazers, the system buckers, the outer-limit thinkers, the so-called rebellious women. They are the women who risked their lives to save others, to tend to others' needs, to care for the good of others. They are the women who saw gaping holes in how this world was being ruled, and understood their call to step up, step in, and stand in their rightful authority to rule.

"Trust in the Lord with all your heart, and lean not on your own understanding; in all your ways acknowledge Him, and He shall direct your paths," (Proverbs 3:5-6 NIV).

Let me lend insight into my own leadership journey. First of all, I will say that I always believed that I had something in me that was "different." I got that I am unique. And so are you. Most of my life has found me set apart and standing out. This was not of my own choosing, but because of God's design. To know me, to really know me, you would know that I am a walking dichotomy between "here am I, send me!" and "who, me?"

My soul is bold, colorful, adventurous, pioneering, exciting and, yes, it has no problem taking charge. It is not afraid to speak up and is confident in all situations. It wants to lead, to move a people and or a process forward. It is progressive, positive, and potential-driven. My soul came here as the purveyor of joy…to lead an exciting life, to make a difference, to make this world a better place. It has the "here am I, send me" spirit.

Not only was I set apart, but God gave me a physical body that could support my soul's desires and purpose. I am a fairly tall woman at over, 5' 7" in my stocking feet. I am statuesque, curvy, and I like to wear high-heeled shoes to events and gatherings, which places me anywhere between 5'10" and 5'11". When I walk into a room, my physical presence can make me known before I utter a word.

Yet, in my mind's eye, for a long time well into my adult years, I saw myself as shy, timid, flawed and unsure of myself. I knew I had skills and talents. I didn't come here to be idle. I knew God had a purpose and a plan for my life, but I preferred to use my skills in the background, in supportive roles, or to work alone. I tried to convince myself that was my place of comfort, my place of service, and where I belonged. But really, it was my hiding place. Whenever I was called out to do something that could be recognized by many, I shivered in my boots because I did not want the responsibility or the attention. Yet, the attention came anyway. And, it happened time after time after time.

Imagine this scene: A group of us is called into a room. They tell us to line up in a horizontal line. They then tell us that we are being considered for a role. Not just any role, but a role that would put any one of us in the spotlight, would require you to lead others, and be responsible for outcomes. It was important that the right candidate be selected. Someone who was fearless, adventuresome and confident. Someone who could look at a problem and see options and probable solutions from A to Z. Someone who could inspire others to be their best selves, do their best work.

Then they ask, "Which one of you, with a little coaching, is ready for this amazing opportunity? Please step forward." I look up and down the line at my obviously qualified peers and shudder, thinking "What am I doing here?" With my feet firmly planted in place, I knew I wasn't going to volunteer. Nope, I'm not moving! And then, I hear my name called. Although I did not step forward, I found that the others had stepped backward. Stunned, I manage to whisper, "Who, me?" The response I hear is "Yes, you."

I suspect many of you find yourselves in this dilemma as well. A bold "here I am, send me" soul that is energized to change the world, to make a difference. Who has heard the leadership call, but has been limited by a culture that has you shaking your head saying, "Who, me?" This is what it felt like in my family structure. This is what it felt like in school. This is what it felt like when I was in the corporate world. This is what it felt like when I was called to ministry. And this is what it felt like when I served in, and was recognized by, the community.

Not knowing that you were fashioned to rule, or that your path is ordered by God, will have you asking the question, "Who, me?"

Prior to the onset of the global pandemic in 2020, there was a sense that the world was in the midst of a course correction. Something was happening that would fundamentally change the trajectory of history, the way we do things, the way we treat people, and who was in charge. I couldn't identify it at the time, but I definitely felt it. And, it had to do with the way the universe had been tended to. Between global warming, oil spills, out of control pollution, animal cruelty, ozone layer issues, and natural resource misuse, it was evident that we have not been good stewards of the earth's resources. We surely had gotten off track and needed to get back on the right path.

Not many months later, in comes the global pandemic that has upended and changed everything. Uncertainty permeated almost every home. Leadership was under scrutiny, challenged in all areas and segments of life. Yet, when we looked to leaders to demonstrate behaviors needed for this present circumstance, we looked for the ones ruling with an iron fist, if you will, because that is what we've seen. That is how we learned. That is what we've been taught is effective. We have seen those behaviors in play. Compassion is rarely used in the same sentence as this form of ruling.

However, in the global pandemic, the old models of leadership clashed with the present need of the people. This played out on the global stage. A shift needed to happen. And the Church did not escape this leadership dilemma.

Let me try to explain. When the global health pandemic, called COVID-19 emerged, church life as we knew it abruptly changed. Without warning, the Church was forced to leave the building. Media teams scrambled to figure out or find technology to continue worship services. Church leaders concerned themselves with how to raise the funds needed to pay bills. How do we keep the children and the elderly connected to the local church body? Pastors and clergy struggled with how to visit the sick, bury the dead and yes, marry folk. Zoom, Microsoft Teams,

Google Hangouts and platforms like these became the new "I see you" of choice.

Around that same time, a "social justice pandemic" on a parallel course converged with the health pandemic. George Floyd made international news. With a knee on his neck, we watched in horror, as he died uttering the now infamous words, "I can't breathe!" This brought an unexpected response—global social unrest. We lent our voices in protest against police brutality, inequality and unfair treatment of black and brown people. We stood with Black Lives Matters demanding justice for folk too numerous to name. No justice, no peace could be heard ringing out from city to city and state to state.

But there was yet another pandemic that the Church also faced, a spiritual one. This virus had been festering and permeating the Church universally, which converged with the other pandemics. All were moving with full, unpredictable force. However, the other pandemics were noisier, demanding immediate attention. We had just enough energy to deal with what was physically in front of us. Yet, the symptoms from the spiritual pandemic were also evident.

In the natural, as the earth was groaning from humankind's faulty rulership of its resources in the air, on land, and under the sea, on a spiritual level, the Church had been dealing with ages of lovelessness, unholy alliances, competition and unforgiveness. We dealt with divisiveness, resource hoarding, and exclusivity. Access to worship was cut off for many—the young, the old, and those with differing thoughts and views—all within the walls of the church buildings. And leadership roles by women were few and far between. Yes, women were being ordained, but not in all denominations. Yes, women were assigned to pastor, but not over major congregations.

Although some of our congregations were asymptomatic, they were exposed to this spiritual virus, nonetheless. This caused the church to lose her zeal for the things of God, relinquish her spiritual power and misplace her love for God and others.

The convergence of the pandemics exposed the leadership gap as across the board, congregations and communities were crying out for the kind of leadership that said, "tend to me," "care for me." The gifts and graces of compassion, nurturing and other characteristically feminine traits is what's needed to restore balance.

We have an unprecedented opportunity to address the spiritual dis-ease within the Church, to ensure that when we go back in, our minds are clear, our hearts are clean and we can be certain that we are focused on the things that God cares about, which is restoring order for the good and the very good. But it's going to take women stepping into leadership with confidence and trusting God for direction, clarity, and the outcomes.

Women, you were fashioned with skills and abilities not just for task number one, which is to populate the world, but also for assignment number two—to rule. When you were created, you were handpicked by God to use the gifts that He placed in you, for this purpose. The gifts of grace are the gift of nurturing, the gift of encouragement, and the gift of compromise. Those are gifts that you are to use when you are in leadership. Those are the gifts leaders need in a post-pandemic society.

All throughout history we have been given warnings as to the consequences of not ruling as God intended. As a matter of fact, the earth itself has been groaning. It's been groaning with our misuse of the environment. It's been groaning with the misuse of natural resources. It has been groaning with the misuse of bodies that have been devalued and cast aside as if they don't matter. The human carnage that has been strewn across global nations as a result of rivalry, greed, and wars, in the name of religion. This has the earth groaning about the blood that has been spilled because humans want to dominate other humans. The earth has been groaning! As if to plead for Jesus' return, or give us ruleHERship that resembles God's original design to restore order.

Women, what you have, in your natural design state, is what is needed to govern now. If this global upheaval has shown us anything, it is showing us that things will never be the same. It's shown that the way we were operating is not sufficient to tend to and rule over the world expanding in self-care or a "soul care" consciousness. That's what we were fashioned to do. That's how we were fashioned to lead.

Women rise up! Understand who you are and how you were made and what you bring to the table. Men, understand that women were designed and fashioned by God from the very beginning to co-lead and co-rule this world. You will not be losing anything by creating spaces for women to co-lead, whether in the board room or the pulpit. As a matter of fact, all will thrive when we include all the gifts of those created in God's image.

All of the philosophes and theologies that say women are subjugated to submissive roles, or subservient to men are not just outdated, they need to be eliminated.

The Voice of Authority and Advocacy

If you were to query most women on whether a woman has the authority to lead, they would probably say, "yes, just not over me," or "just not as my pastor." What determines the authority to create? What gives leadership credibility or not?

When God created the good and very good, it was on authority of His spoken Word. God's voice carried power to create the universe. And since you are made in God's image and likeness, your voice, likewise, carries the authority to create and to rule.

Let's examine your voice. What do you think about it and how do you use it? In order to walk in the authority that you have been given to rule, you need to come to terms with your voice. Here's what I mean.

When I was a young girl, I had something to say. I talked a lot. I raised my hand to answer questions. Others asked me for answers. In my excitement, and sometimes frustration, I would blurt out answers, even when I wasn't recognized to speak. I had something to say. I got in trouble for talking too much, or too long, or out of turn. I remember having to write 'I will not talk' 500 times, several times! Eventually, this led to the errant conclusion that my voice didn't really matter. And it shaped how I saw myself, used my voice, and how I began to interact with others. Treatment like this is how we shake the confidence and creativity of gifted writers, Pulitzer prize winners and great novelists.

One thing this treatment could not do, however, is cancel my love for the written word. That was deep inside of me. You might say that I developed an early love affair with the written word that still stands to this day. When we don't know how to help young people recognize, shape and manage their gifts, they are likely to think they have nothing to offer the planet, and their voice doesn't matter. I'm here to tell you that your voice does indeed matter! It has authority!

In my twenties I heard a call to preach. However, I still was unsure of my voice because of my childhood experiences, so I ignored it. I even went so far as to bargain with God, insisting that I must have been given the wrong assignment. And to prove the point, I continued to work in the church in various positions, and always behind the scenes.

God spoke, and things happened. So, I ask you, what are you speaking? What are you telling yourself about yourself? Is it good? Is it very good? The power of your ruleHERship begins with the power of the words you allow yourself to believe about yourself. Use your voice to remind yourself of who you are, what you have to say, and why you are saying it. God has fashioned you to rule the world, and you can't do it without your voice. You have the voice of authority.

Your voice is not only powerful, but also empowering. Someone is waiting to hear what you have to say. Their very life might depend upon it. Rulership also is advocacy on behalf of the marginalized.

We live in a society that is quick to devalue the lives of people that they fear. That fear is driven by a lack of understanding. We need leaders who are not afraid to subdue the earth. Whether it is revamping laws that strip away human rights or making laws to ensure equity and justice. Using your voice is advocacy.

An Affirmation for Your Voice

I have something to say! In my voice is the power to create. To make sense of the nonsense, to infuse peace where there is disorder, to spread joy where there is none, and to speak hope when all seems lost. My voice is used to encourage others to also use their voice. God fashioned my voice before I was born and gave me the authority to use it. When I rule, it is for the purpose of keeping order of the good and very good.

Conclusion

By now you should see yourself differently, more powerfully. See yourself as God sees you. Use your voice for the good of those who are marginalized by society. Find opportunities and create spaces for shared leadership. We all fare better when order is restored, humankind is carrying out their assignment as intended by God to take care of the earth, and we do it together. You must lead. After all, you were Fashioned by God to Rule the World!

Journal

Fashioned by God to Rule the World

Journal

Fashioned by God to Rule the World

Chapter 5
The PowHER of Holy Rest and Spa

Corine Carter Murphy, MBA

Corine's HERstory

    I am Corine Carter-Murphy, founder and CEO of REDLIPS, and I am *Fashioned by God to Rule the World*. Born in Chattanooga, TN, with a brief stay in San Francisco, CA, I have been married to William L. Murphy since 1987. We are the parents of Kanisha, William, and Minique, and the grandparents of Keyon, TeSean, Peyton and Mallori, all of whom we love and adore. I am a God-fearing woman who is passionate about my relationship with God, as well as encouraging, inspiring and edifying others to see their gifts and use them to the fullest.

    For over thirty-five years Greater Faith Temple (GFT) Missionary Baptist Church has been my church home. There, I was the financial secretary for twenty-five plus years, as well as a member of the choir. I am currently active as the leader of our SHE (Saved-Happy-Elevated) Ministry where "Worship and Work" is our church motto.

In 1987 I began my journey into the corporate arena with a nationally known insurance company. Currently, I serve as a team lead within the Legal Division where I train new employees, assist team members with caseloads, as well as manage a case load of my own to support the mission of the enterprise.

Obtaining my Master's in Business Administration from Kaplan University in 2010, with a specialization in project management and information technology, ignited my entrepreneurial dream. Possessing a Bachelor of Science as well as an associate of science in paralegal studies provided the legal experience relevant to business in the 21st century.

Under the leading of the Holy Spirit, I was led to a historical direct sales company, Traci Lynn Brand, where I use my skills daily to bless others as well as myself. Known for its high fashion, quality jewelry, handbags and accessories, the business afforded me the necessary platform to reach an audience predestined by God before I was even created. I've been blessed to earn paid all-inclusive trips, awards and bonuses, most notably, I earned the name "Cash Carter-Murphy" by a fellow team member and our CEO for becoming the first in the company to earn six-figures in sales in just six months.

In 2016 I birthed REDLIPS (Respected-Empowered-Divas-Living-In-Power-and-Success), and it officially opened for business June 2018. Inspired by the Holy Spirit to "create your own day" I started wearing red lipstick every Friday and posting a picture on social media encouraging women to join me. My passion for how women's lives can be enhanced through fashion, favor, and faith became a priority. The color red can be associated with many things, but when you see REDLIPS I want you to recognize that the color is associated with boldness, the heart and the blood of Jesus.

Chapter 5
The PowHER of Holy Rest and Spa

Thus the heavens and the earth were finished, and all the host of them. And on the seventh day God ended his work which he had made; and he rested on the seventh day from all his work which he had made. And God blessed the seventh day, and sanctified it: because that in it he had rested from all his work which God created and made.
—Genesis 2:1-3

"Like the dew in the morning, gently rest upon my heart, rest Jesus, rest Jesus." Judith Christie McAllister put these lyrics to paper and her songs have resounded with believers for many years. As I listen to her sing, I visualize her in the atmosphere that the lyrics describe. I see a crisp, early spring morning and the sun shining brightly. She is sitting on a porch swing singing, which could have been a form of prayer asking Jesus to take refuge in her heart so that she could avoid any unwelcomed encounters of the day. This is a form of rest, but it is unlike the rest God proclaimed at the beginning of time.

Come with me on a journey as we walk through the most talked about day in Scripture—the seventh day. This day was like no other day for all of mankind. It was established and given a name at its first mention. You and I were there on that day also, because Genesis 1:27 (NKJV) says, "God created man in His own image; in the image, of God He created him; male and female He created them."

In our reading of the text in Genesis 2:2-3, four tasks were manifested by God on the seventh day, that are significant for our lives today. These activities set the model for mankind. Starting with verse 2, we note the first mention of "the seventh day" and it goes on to say that God completed His work. For every beginning there is an end, and for God to have completed His work there had to have been a beginning. That beginning was

Genesis 1:1 which states, "God created the heavens and the earth," and for the next several days God created until the end of day six.

This is similar to my experience working in project management, where all projects are temporary assignments. Each one has a beginning and an end. Whether short-term, lasting one to three days, or long-term, lasting for several years, the dates are established from the onset. With each assignment there are dates aligned to keep us on task and assure the project is completed by a specific date.

The second thing we note in the text is that God rested from His work. How many of us can say that we have rested once we have completed something? Whether in our personal or professional lives, rest is often overlooked. God created a model for us to follow when work has ended. God is God, and He rested. The type of rest God encountered is the type of rest we all should want to experience. Set one day aside to observe as a time of worship. Take the time to be thankful for all of the things accomplished in the days past and rejoice for what lies ahead.

Over the years I have completed many projects, homework assignments, collegiate degrees and even tasks as simple as cooking a meal. Once tasks are completed, a sign of relief wells up on the inside of me and I exhale while seeking the nearest place to rest. I just want to relax and be free from thinking or moving, yet thankful for everything that led up to finishing the project, all while enjoying the moment of completion. This is my reminder of God's rest on the seventh day.

One of the most memorable completions for me was graduation day for my MBA. We were in Miami, FL, a twelve-hour drive from Chattanooga one way, and the weather was beautiful. The keynote speaker was former US Secretary of State Colin Powell. This was such a huge day of accomplishment; I was graduating with a degree that held the key to my future. I shook hands with one of the most prominent men in the country, and my family and I enjoyed a mini vacation at the beach. At the end of the festivities, rest was a priority for me as the day had been full of excitement and accomplishment.

The third point that we can note from our text in Genesis 2:2-3 is that God blessed His work. In other words, He put a stamp of approval on all that He had done. God indicates in Genesis 1:31 (NKJV) that "God saw everything He had made, and indeed it was very good." When one has experienced a sense of satisfaction from completing a goal, we too will give it a stamp of approval indicating this was indeed very good. In today's culture, we can compare this to a celebration.

Merriam-Webster defines the word *blessed* as "of or enjoying happiness" and "honored in worship." God was happy with what He had completed. It was His work and He spoke into existence all that He envisioned and fulfilled. There was nothing left undone, God was indeed happy, justifying the need to bless this day specifically and apart from the previous six days.

Finally, we see in Genesis 2 that God sanctified His work. The seventh day was not like the previous six. In sanctifying His work, the seventh day was given the name "Sabbath" during which there is cessation—or stop—from labor. According to notes taken in the NKJV Women's Study Bible, the seventh day "was not recorded with the evening and morning formula." A suggestion from scholars indicates the continued observance of the Sabbath throughout the history of Israel.

Allow me to be transparent for a moment. While working on this chapter, I will admit that there were some sleepless nights, tears shed, countless hours of reading, studying and some procrastination. There even were times when I could no longer think clear thoughts. I was determined to fulfill my dream no matter what I had to sacrifice. I knew that once all was completed a *sabbatical* or "a break or change from a normal routine" would be on the horizon.

Let us take an in-depth look at the meaning of the words *holy*, *rest* and *spa* individually. Then I will acknowledge how they are brought together for our good. *Holy* is defined as "having a divine quality" or "venerated as or as if sacred." Based on our subject matter, God is the Holy One who possesses these qualities as well as provides the manner in how it should be acknowledged for us all. According to Exodus 20:8 (NKJV) we are to "Remember the Sabbath day, to keep it holy." We recognize this passage as one of the Ten Commandments given by God to Moses for the people of Israel.

Throughout the NKJV Bible, the word holy is referenced 567 times. Based on the significance of the word and its divine meaning, it is to be respected at all times. Regardless of whatever term you place before or after the word holy, you will see God. In my daily meditation, I retreat to my prayer closet where I can have one-on-one time with God; this has become my holy place at home.

The word *rest* has various meanings, but for this purpose we will reference three, with relevant information for the context. Definitions for rest include a) "a freedom from activity or labor," b) "a state of motionlessness or inactivity," and c) "a peace of mind or spirit." It is believed the reference for the first definition best describes God's method of rest on the seventh day. It is noted in Exodus 31:15 (NKJV) "work shall be done for six days, but the seventh is the Sabbath of rest, holy to the Lord."

Over the course of six days, God created everything He envisioned for the heavens and the earth, and all that is within. According to Genesis 1:2 (NIV), "the earth was formless and empty, darkness was over the surface of the deep," until God spoke and said, "Let there be." God's vision was complete in six days, whereas our visions may take longer to complete.

Habakkuk 2:2 (NKJV) states, "Write the vision and make it plain upon the tablets." A dream to become an entrepreneur was placed in my heart at an early age. It was in 2010 after I completed my college degrees that I wrote the vision of success for my life. I can further note Jeremiah 29:11 (MSG) as a driving force in my life, "I know what I'm doing. I have it all planned out—plans to take care of you, not abandon you, plans to give you the future you hope for." My future for REDLIPS (Respected-Empowered-Divas-Living-In-Power-and-Success) began in 2016 when the Holy Spirit birthed it into my life. Now it is available for the world to see.

As the founder and CEO of REDLIPS, it is my mission to "Enhance, Inspire, and Empower Lives" each day. Our vision simply allows us to, "Empower lives across the world, leading to successfully changed lives one generation to the next." My future with REDLIPS in collaboration with the fashion side of my businesses, Jewelz by Traci Lynn, along with Traci Lynn Beauty, are well on their way toward fulfilling the established mission. When a woman is passionate about her God-given gifts, execution is effortless. When you do what you love and love what you do it confirms your call.

The combination of my entrepreneurial pursuits allows me to demonstrate my skills and knowledge related to life, spirituality, and business, and empowerment for my desired audience. This unique blend helps others develop their own spiritual gifts, vision map and board, discover personal empowerment, receive daily encouragement, enter into public speaking and many other self-development activities for their lives.

While REDLIPS has not reached its full potential, we are well on our way. When the time comes for me to sit back on the seventh day of this venture I, too, will follow after the model set by God and *rest* acknowledging my work is good. Until then, I will keep at it. *Fashioned by God to Rule the World* does not mean taking over, it simply means to pull out and exercise the authority of the gifts that God has given.

Looking at my life I see how I allow the busyness of each day to often distract me from rest. As an entrepreneur, wife, mother, employee, businesswoman and leader, my daily schedules oftentimes run into each other, yes, even on the Sabbath day. I often find myself engaged in some form of work whether for my business, my job or something around the house. We as women are always busy. After working on this project, it has become clearer to me that I need to be intentional about rest, and even more so on the Sabbath day.

I should clarify that the term for rest for this purpose is not to be viewed as sleep. Sleep takes on various meanings that do have a role in the context of rest. By comparison, studies show one in three adults lack sleep, however, there are no direct studies on the term rest. Sleep, as it is defined by Merriam-Webster is "the natural, easily reversible periodic state of many living things that is marked by the absence of wakefulness and by the loss of consciousness of one's surroundings." Rest is not that, it is simply peace of mind or spirit.

Studies show less than fifty percent of women actually experience rest. When I see these numbers, several reasons come to mind as to why. Perhaps some do not understand the true meaning or need for rest, others may feel guilty, and then some just do not take the time to rest. But we have established that God rested. He is our example to follow without reservation. If we can keep the activities of the seventh day from Genesis 2:2-3 in our hearts it can become a part of our lives.

Now let's look at the word *spa*. Having no biblical reference, it is often associated with tranquility for the mind, body and soul. Bringing the three terms together—holy, rest and spa—and selecting defining words from each, we can describe them collectively as *"divine freedom for the mind."* This can be implemented into our lives for our good.

Here are some ways in which we can experience holiness, rest and spa:

- Walking in the park, on the beach, or on a nature trail two to three days per week.
- Practice self-care; treat yourself to a manicure and pedicure at least once a month.

- Take a calming, hot mineral bath one to two days a week.
- Turn off social media for two to three hours, one day per week during peak hours.
- Spend time alone with God, daily.

The list can go on, this is just a jumpstart to start you in the direction of experiencing some things for yourself.

Journaling, reading and quiet time in my prayer closet are methods that I use to rest from day-to-day activities of work and business ventures. I choose to categorize the type and length of rest based on the activity. As stated earlier, with the completion of this project a sabbatical is near, which will call for a different type of rest versus journaling, reading or quiet time. This rest will require a change of scenery, away from my normal environment and people for at least three days. I get excited just focusing on the end result of resting.

Words to a song written by gospel pioneer, Rev. Clay Evans say, "As I look back over my life, and I think things over, I can truly say that I've been blessed. I've got a testimony." I feel these are befitting for this chapter writing. God looked back over all He had done. He, too, had a testimony for all of mankind.

Genesis 2:1-3 (MSG) says, *"Heaven and Earth were finished, down to the last detail. By the seventh day God had finished his work. On the seventh day he rested from all his work. God blessed the seventh day. He made it a Holy Day because on that day he rested from work, all the creating God had done."*

Fashioned by God to Rule the World

Journal

Fashioned by God to Rule the World

Journal

Fashioned by God to Rule the World

Chapter 6
Wealth Creation in the Garden

L. Renee Richardson, MBA

L. Renee's HERstory

L. Renee Richardson, MBA, is a founder, CEO and chairman of the board with more than two decades of experience running three global corporations: Women of Vision and Destiny Ministries Worldwide, Wealth and Riches Today Inc. and the I AM Worth It Foundation Inc., headquartered in Chicago, IL with global teams in North America, Asia and coming soon in Africa. Wealth and Riches Today, Inc. is a WBENC certified woman-owned enterprise, placing it in the top .12 percent of the 13.2 million women businesses in the US. They have corporate offices in Chicago and Columbus, GA.

For nearly forty-five years, L. Renee has served at the top levels of corporate, ministry, church, and kingdom arenas, and as an entrepreneurial leader. After serving in church leadership for more than two decades, the Lord called her to lead her own ministry, Women of Vision and Destiny Ministries Worldwide, Inc. (WOVD) through a divine impartation by convening Apostle Dr. Ron Cottle. Throughout her Christian journey, L. Renee has served a number of pastors including Bishop Luther C. Anderson, Bishop Prince James, Bishop A.C. Richards, Bishop Dr. Horace

E. Smith, Bishop D. Rayford Bell, Bishop Warren J. Hoard, Dr. Bill and Veronica Winston, and Bishop L.D. Skinner. She has served in leadership positions in the Living Witnesses of the Apostolic Faith, Pentecostal Assemblies of the World and the Pentecostal Churches of the Apostolic Faith International.

In November 2000, L. Renee was visiting her parents in Columbus, GA, and attended a workshop where Dr. Cottle was teaching about Moses at the burning bush, and purpose and destiny—terms with which she was unfamiliar. After the class, she asked Dr. Cottle to pray for her. Instead, he said he was going to impart. She remembers hearing him say that the anointing that was on him he would place on her. He had everyone in the room point their hands to her and he delivered an impartation. Her whole world changed. WOVD was birthed the next week when L. Renee returned home to Chicago.

Fifteen years later, L. Renee was released into full-time ministry and created WOVD's Vision 20/25 to build sixty-seven women's centers and LOVED Academies with the goal of touching the lives of 4 billion women. After moving back to Columbus in July 2019 to care for her aging parents, Dr. Cottle ordained L. Renee and her husband Glen as pastors.

L. Renee serves as the worldwide senior pastor of Women of Vision and Destiny Ministries Worldwide, Inc. which celebrates twenty-one years of educating, empowering, and enlightening 1.2 million women worldwide. With a powHERful global teaching pastoral team, WOVD has a WOVD TV social media presence on four continents (North America, Asia, Africa, and Australia) and audiences in India, Cameroon, China, Mexico, The Bahamas, Zambia, Papua New Guinea, United States, Nigeria, Malaysia, Taiwan, Philippines, Uganda, Pakistan, Canada, South Africa, Jamaica, Syria, Sierra Leone, and Kenya. L. Renee and her team are seen weekdays on the *Power Up Your Faith Show* on Facebook.

A credentialed intercessor by Living World Christian Center and Dr. Bill Winston, L. Renee loves to spend time with

God. She reads the Bible daily and has walked through the entire Bible over twenty times since 2000, a practice she learned from Dr. Horace E. Smith. She loves the Lord and spending time with Him in her prayer closet, as well as hosting mountain top prayer retreats. Her prayers have extended the lives of her husband, mother, and father all of whom were attacked by strokes.

Known as the Billionaire Visionnaire, L. Renee served as a media director, and the third highest-ranking woman of color, at the world's largest advertising and communications companies. During her twenty-year career, she managed $1 billion in advertising for Fortune 100 clients.

L. Renee and her husband took a leap of faith and left the corporate world to live their dream of business ownership. Together they opened a Marble Slab Creamery ice cream shop franchise on Michigan Avenue, which remained open for six years. The store served 1.2 million multi-cultural ice cream lovers and employed 100 young people, many of them inner-city youth, who learned the ropes of becoming leaders. The store was on the local and national news and visited by the mayor of Chicago, local aldermen and sports celebrities.

After the business closed in 2012 and Glen had a massive cerebral hemorrhage, L. Renee went through a dark season and spent hours in her prayer closet, rebuilding her mind, body, and soul. During that time, she literally re-invented herself and shaped her destiny. Inspired by a story in the Bible in 2 Kings 4 about the prophet Elijah and the widow heavily in debt, L. Renee designed her I AM Worth It Story, discovered her pot of olive oil, and turned it into an oil field.

Chapter 6
Wealth Creation in the Garden

And the LORD God planted a garden eastward in Eden; and there he put the man whom he had formed. And out of the ground made the LORD God to grow every tree that is pleasant to the sight, good for food.
—Genesis 2:8-9a

My first memories of wealth are from my childhood. I remember a medium-sized green, plastic Tupperware bowl where I kept my funds. My parents would give me money and I put it in this bowl. I have vague images of monies going in and out of it. I honestly have no idea what became of the green bowl but understanding wealth has impacted my life. I have been blessed to earn over $1 million in the corporate and business worlds. I have spent the last eight years studying how to create a $1 million dollar a year enterprise. I have developed a proprietary system called "Seven Steps to Seven Figures."

I remember a powerful question posted on social media about how young a child should be before she is taught about money. I said two or three years old. If we can potty train her, we can teach her about money. Do you remember your first experience with wealth? Let us look at the first book in the Bible to get insights on the beginnings of wealth. It is a powerful revelation.

God is a Master Gardner

The Bible begins the story of the creation of mankind with a powerful lesson on wealth. God is a Master Gardener. He planted the most beautiful garden in the world. It was called Eden. Some scholars believe that a better interpretation is that there was a garden in Eden. I love reading modern magazines like *Architectural Digest* which features some of the most beautiful and incredible gardens in the world. One of the Seven

Wonders of the Ancient World is the Hanging Gardens of Babylon.

There are two accounts of how the Hanging Gardens of Babylon came into existence. Both legends involve women. According to Wikipedia, "the garden was built by King Nebuchadnezzar, who ruled the city for forty-three years starting in 605 BC. According to accounts, the gardens were built to cheer up Nebuchadnezzar's homesick wife, Amyitis. She was the daughter of the king of the Medes and was married to Nebuchadnezzar to create an alliance between the two nations. The land she came from, though, was green, rugged, and mountainous, and she found the flat, sun-baked terrain of Mesopotamia depressing. The king decided to relieve her depression by recreating her homeland and building an artificial mountain with rooftop gardens."

The second account cited in the Encyclopedia Britannica is that the gardens were built by the Assyrian Queen Semiramis during her five-year reign starting in 810 BC. Both stories involve women and our love for greenery and the beauty of a garden. Gardens are created to manifest the power of creation.

My Parents Were Gardeners

My parents were gardeners in their fifties and sixties. I have no idea how they were able to work full-time jobs and build a garden in our backyard. It is amazing what older generations have been able to get done without the distraction of social media. My parents' yard is one and a half acres, comparable to the amount of land on which we now build ten to fifteen houses. The backyard was about 100 by fifty feet wide.

I was about thirteen years old when my parents had their dream home built from the ground on their land. I remember so many different products came from the garden. I remember the big watermelons we carried from the garden in a wheelbarrow. The watermelons were sweet and juicy. My parents were so good at gardening, that they expanded their garden to the lot next door to our house.

I remember my dad tilling the land with a robust machine that was designed to break up the grass. Ironically, I did not go outside to the garden. I was not attracted to dirt and bugs. My role was child labor. My assignment was to pick the beans and wash the greens and squash. My grandmother would also pick beans. I loved the watermelons and tomatoes the best. We would make tomato and mayonnaise sandwiches.

Now I realize that the garden was a wealth creator. According to Statista, it is estimated that in 2019, the gardening industry generated a combined total revenue of just over 99 billion US dollars, with an average spend of 503 US dollars per household, on lawn care and gardening activities. Now that I oversee my parents' estate, I can see that lawn care is an extremely profitable business. We spend nearly $4,000 a year having my parents' lawn manicured.

By employing the techniques of successful farming, my parents produced a crop that could generate wealth. In Georgia during the summer, we would see roadside stands featuring fresh fruit from the orchards for sale. My parents could have sold their produce, but instead they gave it away. My mom would take the fruit and "can" or "preserve" it by putting it in mason jars and storing it in the pantry.

When visitors would stop by, as they often did, my parents would pack them a goody bag of fresh vegetables and fruit preserves made from peaches and especially figs. We still have a humongous fig tree in our backyard. My mom would ask her mother how to make preserves. Our celebrity guests included Bishop Charles E. Poole, founder and presiding Bishop of the Living Witnesses of the Apostolic Faith, and Bishop Luther C. Anderson. I remember mom giving them lots of garden-grown products to take back home and share with their families. Wealthy women share.

Genesis tells us that God planted the Garden of Eden eastward. I know this was strategic. God is a master strategist. Everything has significance. According to real estate experts, the first and second choices for homes are north and east facing.

Our Chicago home faced east where the sun would come directly into our bedroom. I believe it faced eastward to allow for optimal sunshine. We know that sunlight is essential. I remember when I started my career in Chicago, I noticed a dark spot on my neck. I made my doctor's appointment and he told me that it was because of lack of sunlight. Ironically, one of the reasons that I left the South was to get away from too much sunlight that contributed to headaches. I would feel faint and go inside to avoid the intense southern heat. Today, we hear about the importance of vitamin D which comes from sunshine.

Our Journey to Financial Freedom

The Lord gave me a revelation of wealth in 2013 that transformed my mind and inspired me to rename my company from Leap of Faith University to Wealth and Riches Today. This revelation is found in Psalm 112. I found this scripture in the heart of an extremely dark season.

In 2006, my husband and I set a path to business ownership and financial freedom. We had always been in the six-figure world. It was my husband's desire to own a business. I preferred being able to turn the lights off and go home. Ironically in 2004 I taught my first entrepreneurship class for Women of Vision and Destiny Ministries Worldwide, Inc. (WOVD). I used my mentor Cheryl Broussard's book *Sister CEO* and taught about twenty women in my home for four weeks. It was during this class, that I asked God what was my business? He said WOVD! Jesus said He was about his Father's business.

As the pressures of corporate America grew, promotion opportunities were slim to none—despite me accomplishing incredible feats and asking repeatedly to be promoted to vice president. My eyes turned toward entrepreneurship. One day while lying on the sofa, during a six-week recovery from an illness, I realized how unappreciated I was by my director. While I was out sick, I received no phone calls and no flowers. My desire grew to own a business and build the WOVD center. I prayed with my caregiver—I'd asked the hospital to refer a woman of color to help me heal. In the world of miracles, shortly after our prayer, the Lord opened a $100,000 financial door. I later learned from the bank that this type of offering did not exist. Now I know that my desires pulled the financing out of the spirit realm into the natural realm. I was employing garden principles.

We were successful employees in corporate America. My husband is a restaurant management guru, and I am a strategic business and finance expert. We believe we are a powerful combination. We celebrated twenty-five years of marriage in May 2021.

We chose Marble Slab Creamery as our franchise option to build out on Michigan Avenue in Chicago. I discovered the concept in Columbus, GA. When I tasted the premium ice cream and delicious fresh baked waffle bowl, covered with white chocolate, I said aloud, "I am bringing this franchise to Chicago." I sent off for the paperwork and kept it in the dream file until the fullness of time. We purchased two franchises for $60,000 plus eight percent royalties. The first location we selected was a brand-new retail space in Chicago's hottest market, the South Loop.

When we started, our mindset was not on Michigan Avenue, the city's wealthiest shopping district. Our mindsets were at a California and Garfield level, a lower-income area located on the Southside near Englewood, one of Chicago's toughest communities. Believe it or not, the retail owner rejected us because they did not want a restaurant business. At least that's what they said. Ironically, within a few years, they built a Subway franchise.

Fashioned by God to Rule the World

We lived in Bronzeville and drove down Michigan Avenue every day to get to my corporate office on Wacker Drive. One day I noticed a new retail space on the corner of Michigan about a block from Roosevelt. The realtor was the Lord's Companies and John Mark was the real estate agent. I believed the Lord was sending us a sign.

They approved us for the new retail space in the South Loop without a credit check. We told them it was a franchise. I negotiated 120 days of free rent and we received about $40,000 in build out monies. At the time, I was working full-time as a media director. I wrote a business plan and completed the financial lending paperwork during the early hours of the morning and the evening hours. My body was on autopilot. Our credit was so high, I think we only had one bill that showed up late. I am sure it was an oversight.

I wrote a strategic business plan that resulted in us being awarded a small business loan of over $300,000. I learned that only two percent of African Americans were awarded this type of loan. Less than four percent of capital is awarded to women. Through my Rich Gurlz Club and Rich Color Gurlz Club Inc. Coaching programs I share with women business owners how to negotiate pricing for retail space, write a business plan, build and restore credit, and live their rich, big dreams today.

We were open for six years. We hired an architect and built out the retail space from the ground up. My husband hired the staff. He managed the store, and I continued working in corporate America for another two years before leaving to live my dream life. The store served 1.2 million multi-cultural ice cream lovers and employed 100 young people, many of them inner-city youth, who learned the ropes of becoming leaders. The store was on the local and national news and visited by the mayor of Chicago, local aldermen and sports celebrities. Then the Great Recession of 2008 hit. We felt the impact as thousands lost their jobs and businesses closed.

After our business closed, my husband went back to work and had a massive cerebral hemorrhage. I went through an incredibly dark season and spent hours in my prayer closet, rebuilding my mind, body, and soul. In my prayer closet, God taught me how to re-invent myself, and re-shaped my destiny. Inspired by a story in the Bible in 2 Kings 4 about the prophet Elijah and the widow who was heavily in debt, I designed my I AM Worth It Story®, discovered my pot of olive oil, and turned it into an oil field. I share my discovery in my best-selling book, *The Widow Oil Tycoon: Ten Keys to Turn Your Pot of Oil into an Oil Field,* which is available on Amazon.

Here is the revelation that shifted my mindset:

Blessed are those who fear the LORD, who find great delight in his commands. Their children will be mighty in the land; the generation of the upright will be blessed. Wealth and riches are in their houses, and their righteousness endures forever.
—*Psalm 112:3*

First, the scripture uses the terms wealth and riches. Psalm 112 declares that wealth and riches are a promise to the righteous. It is a reward to those who fear the Lord. To fear the Lord is to reverence Him. According to YourDictionary.com, reverence is defined as deep respect. An example of reverence is when you show deep and complete respect for the Bible as the Word of God. The person this scripture speaks of finds great delight or has pleasure in God's commands. They are delighted to serve Him. The promise then extends to her children. They will be mighty or rulers and leaders in the land. The psalmist implies that when we reverence and delight in God, our lives are filled with wealth and riches. Reading this created an "aha" moment for me.

I learned that my wealth and riches (substance, intellect, leadership teams, and numbers) were manifestations of righteous living. I later realized that our business closing did not impact my wealth. It took me years to come to this revelation. Wealth is in your spirit—your internal self. If I were reverencing God, making

Him the priority in my life, delighting in His Word daily, wealth and riches would become apparent only if I became wealthy on the inside, and did the work that produces wealth and riches.

So, I asked, why wasn't I seeing this manifestation in my life? I read Malachi 3:10.

"Bring ye all the tithes into the storehouse, that there may be meat in mine house, and prove me now herewith, saith the LORD of hosts, if I will not open you the windows of heaven and pour you out a blessing, that there shall not be room enough to receive it."

I paid tithes and offerings since childhood. When the business closed, our income plummeted and everything we owned was in jeopardy for years. Our income went from $325,000 a year to $12.50 an hour in retail. I took a job earning only that much. I figured that if I could run a retail restaurant, I could become a district manager for a top women's fashion store. Despite my efforts to elevate to a management position, I was denied repeatedly. Three years and thirty online applications later, I was still stuck in the $12.50 an hour job. Our faith kept my husband and I showing up in court over forty times fighting for our business and our home. While we let the business go, we kept our house for ten years and finally sold it in the pandemic.

By then, I understood the revelation of the power of visualization. My clients told me the results they received from the principles God taught me in my prayer closet. I took a picture in front of the store's sign and saved it on my cell phone screen. At the beginning of the year, I sent a text to my district manager stating that I was the next general manager of a store. *Wealth and riches are in my house.* Within six months, I was promoted to a general manager in Chicago's exclusive Lincoln Park area.

God began to teach me how to speak and prophesy "wealth and riches are in my house" despite the bills, the red letters, and the court summons that grew to a stack of paper that was an inch thick. They came in daily, and like a flood the Lord lifted a standard against them. I stopped opening mail.

Still, there were no signs of manifestation for what I was believing. Looking back now, I can see that these words, pictures, and thoughts were principles employed in the Garden in Eden. Everything I that I needed to turn my life around, was already in me. I am the Garden. I would write these words on my bills. *The Lord is my Shepherd, I am not in lack.* Though we were walking through the valley of the "shadow" of financial death, and I was fearing the evil of losing our home and losing my husband who suffered an illness, I kept confessing, moving, and seeking first the kingdom of God.

Correlation of Earthly Wealth and Time with God

If we had to measure reverence by time spent with God through His Word, we would readily discover that there is a biblical famine in our country. Only three-quarters of Christians say they believe the Bible is the Word of God. About a third of Americans say they read Scripture at least once a week, while forty-five percent seldom or never read Scripture, according to 2014 data from the Pew Research Religious Landscape Study.

I have a wonderful spiritual discipline that I have employed for more than twenty years. I want to encourage you to do the same and watch your life change amazingly. I read through the entire Bible in a year. I started this in 2000 and the Lord blessed me to create Women of Vision and Destiny Ministries, Inc. I believe planting the Word into my heart, mind, body, and soul opened the heavens for me to be ready to accept the call to minister to 4 billion women worldwide. The spiritual enrichment tool that I use now allows me to walk through the Old Testament once, the New Testament twice, Proverbs twelve times and Psalms twice on an annual basis. I added journaling the Scriptures to my daily reading during my dark season.

The Word literally reads like billboards to my soul. Revelation after revelation after revelation. We now have the Daily Word 365 in WOVD. We have a calendar for women to read through the Bible in a year. Women are not to live by bread alone but by every Word that precedes out of the mouth of God.

I believe it was this spiritual discipline of daily living with God that sustained me when the garden looked like it was not going to bloom. It was a shaky season. When things looked like they were stabilizing, the next thing I knew the rug was snatched from under us. *The Lord is my Shepherd, I am not in lack.* I kept confessing this, not knowing then that I was planting seeds of breakthrough that were taking root in my soul.

How did Eden get its name? According to the Encyclopedia Britannica the term Eden likely derived from the Akkadian word *edinu,* borrowed from the Sumerian *eden,* meaning "plain." I was sitting in my own "plain," building my own life with my words and thoughts.

According to Scienceing.com, Coastal plains form significant terrain connecting large bodies of water with inland regions. Some of the better-known examples of plains include the Atlantic and Gulf coastal plains of North America and the inland coastal plain of Israel and the Mediterranean Sea. Today these sprawling geographic regions are highly populated and have important social and economic functions in addition to their geography.

God gave Adam the best real estate on the planet. Real estate along water sources is highly valued. Waterfront properties are in higher demand. People are willing to pay large sums of money to be in exclusive riverfront and oceanfront properties. I plan to live in houses across the world's finest beaches. I have travelled extensively in the US and abroad and the most gorgeous properties are those by the water. I love land development. God has provided everything that was needed in the Garden in Eden.

The BBC reported that Iraq's marshlands, which lie in the confluence of the Tigris and Euphrates rivers, are believed to be the inspiration for the Bible's Garden in Eden. The wetlands spread 3,500 square miles and support about forty different species of birds. The marshes are a paradise for wildlife. The waters are beautifully still.

Fashioned by God to Rule the World
Are You in Your "Put" Place?

Genesis says that God put man in the Garden. Man was *put* in his set place. Your garden is your set or ordained place where wealth is created almost automatically. I love to write. I write daily. I read the Word of God and journal its meaning and implications. Writers write. I began to rebuild a company based on what I loved to do. I love to travel. I love to teach. I love to empower women economically. During my pitch-black season, I designed the life that I now live! I love entertaining. I love homes. I love spas. I love land development. We hosted our Rich Gurlz Club LuXury Business SPA Retreat at The Henderson Resort in Destin, Florida. It was the resort owned by black woman billionaire Sheila Johnson. It was on the beautiful ocean front. And it was a brand-new resort. I like new things.

This year the Lord said to focus on my company Rich Gurlz Club and publishing. In ninety days, we created a company with forty diverse authors from across the United States. I am living my dream life. We host our L. Renee LuXury Rich Gurl Club Inc. Spa Weekenders at the Hotel Indigo Riverfront in Columbus, GA. It just opened in February. I like new resorts and hosting weekenders for women in business, ministry, and corporate America, where I and our Rich Gurlz Club gurus train. We enjoy the luxury spas and rejuvenate our hearts, minds and souls while working on growth strategies to build seven-figure companies.

Who Can Find a Wealthy Woman?

My mom earned a doctorate in ministry under Dr. Ron Cottle's schools. She would tell me of the wonderful classes that he offered and how much she learned. She invited me to attend his Hebrew and Greek class. The course came with five books and one of my favorite ministry tools, the Hebrew Greek Key Word Study Bible. This Bible allows you to use the Strong's Hebrew Dictionary of the Old Testament. Wealth comes from the Hebrew word Chayil (#2428). According to Strong's Concordance, wealth means force of men, means or other resources. An army, wealth, virtue, valor, strength, able, activity, army band of men (soldiers), riches, strong, substance, train, valiant. A masculine noun, meaning strength wealth, army. It is the basic idea of strength and influence, and righteous behavior.

When describing women, it speaks of virtuous character. Proverbs 31:10 says, "Who can find a virtuous woman? for her price is far above rubies. The word virtuous is the same word as wealth – Chayil (#2428).

One of my favorite modern day wealthy women of color is Nigeria's Folorunso Alakija who is sixty-eight years old. She is one of the world's 100 richest women. She is a Christian who links her business with serving God. According to *Forbes*, her estimated net worth is $1.1 billion in US dollars. She is an African billionaire businesswoman. She has interests in the fashion, oil, real estate, and printing industries. She is the group managing director of The Rose of Sharon Group which consists of The Rose of Sharon Prints & Promotions Limited, Digital Reality Prints Limited and the executive vice-chairman of Famfa Oil Limited. She also has a majority stake in DaySpring Property Development company. She is an inspiration for wealthy women today.

Fashioned by God to Rule the World

Journal

Fashioned by God to Rule the World

Journal

Fashioned by God to Rule the World

Chapter 7
The Suitable Wife

Kimberly Coleman, BSW, MSW

Kim's HERstory

  Mrs. Kimberly Coleman was born in the small historic town of Tuskegee, AL. She currently resides in Opelika, AL. She is the wife to her wonderful husband Terry, and they have five beautiful children together (Terri, Tracy, Zaria, Hailey, and Isaiah). Kim takes pride in her love for and relationship with God, her family, her zest for life, and her strong work ethic.

  After deciding to retire from more than twenty years in the beauty industry as a successful cosmetologist, she received her bachelor's degree in social work from Troy University. From there she developed a passion for geriatrics. She is currently pursuing her master's degree in social work. Kim plans to use her degree to help cultivate and establish change and initiate importance in the lives of older adults, as well as be a liaison in the kingdom of God by serving the "whole man."

  Kim has always known that entrepreneurship was a part of her life. She lives by the motto that she coined for herself after she lost what seemed to be the career of her dreams in marketing. Because work was such a "big deal" in her life losing her job left her despondent. She was in an unfamiliar, scary place that she had never been in before and was asking God what to do, and where to go. He took her to Romans 12:3. Rebirth happened, and the phrase "Working My Measure" pushed her into another avenue of purpose. Among the many hats she wears alongside her husband, she is an agent for the illustrious company known as JEWELZ by Traci Lynn. This opportunity was truly given by the Lord and has been a blessing in so many areas since day one.

Kim also is the CEO and creator of a Christian-based Facebook blog entitled Motivational Monday where she encourages others to see themselves through the eyes of the Savior and remind them that with God all things are possible. Her social media messages of hope and encouragement push those who embrace them to another level of worth in the kingdom of God. Through her blog, Kim and her husband have birthed Brunch with Terry and Kim. This show gives an in-depth, raw and realistic view of marriage. They connect with their viewers by sharing what God has taught them on how to make their marriage work.

Kingdom service has always been a passion for Kim, and she knew in her heart from childhood that God had a purpose, plan, and call on her life. She is a member of Harvest Impact Center (HIC) under the leadership of Pastor Ivory Davis. Kim serves as minister, personal relations director, and on HIC's core management team.

Kim gives all honor to the Savior for all that she has been through. These things groomed her to become the person that she is today. Her favorite scripture explains it perfectly: Psalm 119:71 (MSG), "My troubles turned all out for my best. They forced me to learn from your book."

Chapter 7
The Suitable Wife

And the Lord God said, it is not good that the man should be alone; I will make him an help meet for him.
—Genesis 2:18

Most women that I know look for the American Dream—to become an adult, pursue a great education, land a dream job, meet Mr. Right, fall in love, and get married. This sequence of events can be seen in movies, heard in stories and songs, and instilled from generation to generation. It is all around us. Two people falling hopelessly in love and living happily ever after is the goal. However, it does not always happen that way. Even if you go after it, most times this dream never seems to just fall into place. And if it does happen, the way life and marriage have been portrayed in our minds is very different from reality. Why is this the case?

I can say from my personal journey and experiences that most times we jump into relationships without searching things out. It is almost like putting together a bicycle or a piece of furniture. It's true, you may get it together without reading all of the instructions, but it will take more time, sweat, and tears when the manual would have been a big help. There may even be parts or pieces that we leave out that are supposed to complete the project. Or sometimes, we get frustrated and overwhelmed with the process, never get it put together, and stop trying. A lot of times, and for a lot of reasons, we do not read the manual or search out proper instruction.

Marriage was instituted from the beginning of creation. God even saw fit for every animal and creature to have a mate. In all of this, sometimes I wonder do we really understand what marriage is and the purpose for it? The Lord created marriage for companionship, for creation, to be a help, to complement, to balance, and so much more.

In the book of Genesis, the Lord knew that Adam was going to need someone to be beneficial to him as he carried out the duties of his God-given assignment. In the journey of this thing called life, whether we want to admit it or not, we need companionship of some kind. We were created to coexist. The Lord also knew that this companionship could not be with just any being. This being had to be designed exclusively with Adam in mind. This being had to have one major characteristic—to be *suitable* for Adam. Just like God looked out for Adam, the same goes for you. There is already an "Adam representative" designed, orchestrated, and developed with you in mind. All you must do is be in position—a position of readiness and to be found.

In Proverbs 18:22, it specifically tells us that we are not only to be found but it is a good thing, and in our finding, there is opportunity for the man to gain favor. You are an important part of the plan that completes a dynamite duo. Imagine this—there will be some things that will happen in your marriage just because of you being you. Favor, as I have been told and seen firsthand, carries weight. It is more valuable than money. Favor can manifest opportunities that the ordinary only dream of. That is why understanding the role of being a wife is imperative. Being a wife is a place of position. And do you want to know how to get in this position? It is this simple—get busy finding you!

Let us just think about how Adam must have felt in the garden visualizing everything that he named have their own, appropriate match. Every living creature had their ideal partner, but no one was there for his companionship. I choose to think that would have been a lonely time for him. Just imagine, you have dominion over everything but not having anyone to enjoy it with. There was a deficiency there that needed repair. I believe God saw this in Adam, because He stated that it was not good for man (mankind) to be alone. He also said that in the making of the helper for Adam, it must be a suitable one, one that would coincide with Adam like none other. When Eve was presented to Adam after God created her from his rib, he knew when he saw her that she was the one for him. He named her woman, he knew she was a part of him, and decreed that they were now one.

Have you ever heard any man tell the story of meeting his wife or seeing her from across a crowded room? Often, upon seeing her, he immediately said, "Wow, I am going to marry that woman!" That is the same reaction Adam had when he saw Eve for the very first time. He did not just look at her, he saw Eve in her wholeness—not her perfection. She was a complete being for the role of wife for Adam, and he felt the oneness without it even having to be explained by God. He knew that there was something inside of this woman that no other creation had and that it was perfectly designed from him, for him. He saw her wholeness and it was indeed good!

I had to learn that being whole and finding myself had nothing to do with perfection. No matter how hard I tried, I never perfected being the "perfect" wife. It was not in a meal that I cooked, or how I made the bed, or even on an intimate level. Now all these things are good, but it is not the total package for making marriage a success. I had to get busy finding myself, the real me that was there all the time, I was just apprehensive to pull her out. I had to realize that my uniqueness was on purpose, for a purpose. I had to discover who I was and who God created me to be and above all, I had to embrace it. Then I could see myself in a way I had never seen before.

I discovered things I liked, what I did not like, I uncovered my passions, and took time to fall in love with me first, flaws and all. I forgave myself for so many things I had done, so many decisions I had made that I was not proud of. I recounted the past failures and my deficiencies in a marriage I was previously in, that ended in divorce. Most of all, I began seeing myself through the eyes of the Father. He said that I was the apple of His eye and there was nothing that could separate me from His love.

Wow, that was a wakeup call. I had always said it as a cliché, that God loved me, but now I believed it. I walked in it.

God loves me and you with all that we are. That is when my self-love as well as self-worth flourished. My self-worth was not predicated on the opinion or accolades of others, but it was in the healing love of Jesus! That was a life changing experience. An experience that took work.

I was busy, but in a good way. Busy operating in my current assignment of relearning, restructuring, and rebuilding. Not long after I began that process, I met my husband Terry at a high school football game. He later told me that when he saw me walk into the stadium, he said to himself, "there she is, my wife." When I really stepped into becoming a suitable wife, I was already busy in becoming me! Believe it or not, the last thing on my mind at that time was marriage. I was just busy in the assignment for that season in my life. For me, it was to become the best mother possible.

There are so many examples of being busy with your assignment in the Word of God. When Isaac's servant saw Rebekah, she was drawing water. When Jacob saw Rachel, she was tending to her father's sheep. When Boaz saw Ruth, she was working in the grass field. They were attending to the things that had nothing to do with becoming a wife but was their assignment for that moment. However, it still caught the attention of the one that was already made for them. In all of these instances, those men knew without a shadow of a doubt that those ladies were their mates.

After I began to read and study the concept of suitability, I had what a very well-known talk show host says often when they stumble onto some groundbreaking news; I had an "aha moment." I believe that there is a part that we miss in the pursuit of suitability that is so important. I was learning the purpose of marriage, beginning to understand the role of a wife, getting busy finding myself, and becoming complete, though not perfect.

I thought this was the final piece to the puzzle. This self-work, as a matter of fact, was just the beginning of what it would take to become suitable. Let us go back to Adam. Yes, God knew

Adam needed someone. Adam was feeling inadequate and needed companionship. God said that He would create and present someone suitable for Adam. Adam was put into a deep sleep where God performed the first surgery and removed a rib to use for Eve's creation. Then after the creation, God presented Eve to Adam.

I have read this passage so many times but just recently discovered a very important point. Adam had to acknowledge that Eve was the one. This is something so small but it has a big meaning. Adam confirmed Eve. He spoke over her and established just who she was in his life. He gave her placement. He gave her dominion. He prophesied their unity. He set her apart from any and everything and then set the standard for all others that were to come after him and take on this great journey of two becoming one.

This taught me that even though it may seem outdated and underrated, your suitability does not come from you at all but from the one who finds you suitable. When the man finds you, he affirms you. You know how it goes—he will let everyone know that you are his lady. He establishes the covenant by asking you to marry him. His love for you and his desire to live life with you for the rest of your days sets the tone for all the world to see.

Let me explain further. I am a firm believer in the establishment that God designed. The man was created first. He was given dominion. He was created to provide and work the land and subdue it. He is a bloodline leader whether he realizes it or not. The male species was designed to give order and speak dominance. One of the biggest downfalls is that many men do not even know the power they possess. Adam was given the authority to name everything because God designed it that way. He even named the helper that was given to him.

We must understand that even though we have a responsibility to develop ourselves it is not all for marriage, it is strictly for you. The suitability takes place when that man sees your wholeness and notices that it matches his dominion. God stated that Eve was to be a helper to Adam. How can we help anyone if we are not together? How can we push forth the best in our mate if we are broken and constantly need encouragement? How can we totally surrender our will to God to function in the role of a wife if we do not even know our purpose or why we are on this earth? How can we compromise without comprehension? These are questions I had to ponder in my own busy moments of finding me.

I think most of our time is spent trying to fit into what we think others expect instead of who we truly are. This behavior creates a ride on a hamster wheel of never-ending disappointments. I have definitely had my share. I realized that I based all my happiness on the emotions of others. I tried to become what was expected and not walk in my truth. When the Bible tells us that the truth will make you free, boy does it ever. There is a place in freedom that is indescribable.

Now, back to your busy place. Ladies, we have mastered the art of giving our all to everyone but ourselves. We give to our parents, friends, careers, then to our significant others without even giving it a second thought. Just like the man was created with the strength to lead, we were created with the power to nurture. We love past pain and disappointment, in hopes that one day that spark of all we give will be reciprocated in the same way to us. We expect others to love us just as we have loved them. We bounce back fast and can make it look easy. For better or worse, we can take a licking and keep on ticking, which at times can be a blessing and a curse.

I found out in my own path of self-discovery that we do this because we want to show others how we want to be loved. It is birthed out of a broken place or a part that is unfulfilled most times, especially if you never received a complete love from birth to adulthood. It is a cry out to the one that matters the most in your life, telling what you feel you need from them to make your life complete. That is why it is so important to work on you first. When you try to love out of a place of emptiness, most times the person that is along for the ride with you will become a casualty of war. The war is between the version of you that you created, the person you really are, and your emotions.

I remember blaming guys for not making me feel complete or not loving me the way that I wanted because in my mind I showed them how to do it by the way I treated them. Then I got frustrated and wondered what the problem was. I asked myself these questions: Don't they get me? Don't they see what I need? Do they really love me? What can I do better? How can I change? Before I could really get to the root of the issue, I moved on to the next relationship, and the hamster wheel began to spin again. Sound familiar?

Another aspect is to take accountability for yourself and your growth process. Become just as involved in yourself as you were in all of the other people and situations that you made a priority. Do some sincere praying and meditation and allow the Lord to give you instruction and answer your questions. Let the Word of God assist you in showing you who you are—good, bad, and indifferent.

Taking accountability is a step that sometimes starts out hard but ends up beautiful. It adds strength for the journey. No one can divide and conquer your life like you. As I stated earlier, God did establish man as a leader, but He placed a mechanism on the inside of woman that makes us unstoppable! There also is a leader on the inside of all of us. Man can lead the order, but women lead the way. We are so resilient. We can take a little something and turn it into much. We think quick on our feet. We have the power to build up or tear down. Not only should we take accountability for what we are not proud of, but also for the things that we can do. Being busy finding you is the greatest accomplishment that you could ever achieve!

Although self-discovery early on can help in so many ways, being busy finding you does not only apply to first-time relationships or marriages. It is an evolving and ever-changing system. I remarried at the age of forty-three. Starting a new life meant I had to begin again. Rediscovering who I was for the new journey took the same process. Never feel like time, age, or starting over has counted you out. God gives us grace for everything that we encounter. No one knows what the future holds. We can just rest in the fact that we know Who holds the future. He already knows what we will go through and has already prepared the way.

Having confidence in this is an insurance policy to secure you in the process. Once it all begins to fall into place and you see the transition happen, you see the hand of God moving in your life, you gain that spark and knowledge of who you were created to be, you can see yourself becoming…and then the magic happens. You stand tall, fix that crown, and take on the challenges before you.

I have heard so many times before that it is not how you start but how you finish. Can you agree with me that most of us have had some bumpy starts? When gold is purified it is a very messy, hot, and tedious process. But the value of it increases after the purifying. Your value is increasing. There are things that you have on the inside of you that are priceless. Just like diamonds, the clearer the stone the more it is worth. Find you and be clear and concise on where you want to go.

From this day forward, I will declare that we will rule the world in all of the things that we do. Whether it be marriage, motherhood, at our workplace, and in every arena of our lives. Continue to uncover the winner that dwells on the inside. Walking in the call of a suitable wife is an extension of being a dynamic, whole you. It is time to get busy. Your Adam is looking for you. Be in position. Your future awaits!

Journal

Fashioned by God to Rule the World

Journal

Fashioned by God to Rule the World

Chapter 8
The Woman's Enemy

Crystal Wilhoite, B.S.

Crystal's HERstory

Crystal Wilhoite is a native of Chicago who recently transplanted to the DC area. Professionally, she works with the government performing program and project management on global public health issues. She is a life-long learner and has traditionally led teams and created strategy in highly regulated industries. Before moving into the government sector, Crystal worked in the biopharma and biotech industry. Her research has been recognized and she is published as a first author in the National Academy of Sciences of the United States Journal.

Crystal is the founder and CEO of Inspired Biological Solutions, a network geared towards the professional development of Christians by training them to hear the voice of God for personal and scientific breakthrough.

As an overcomer of abuse, Crystal is passionate about women and children's issues. She serves on the board of nonprofits and is actively engaged at the local level to support these causes. She believes strongly in providing resources and awareness to these issues not only in the community but in the church. Frequently she hosts and co-hosts conferences and educational events to provide practical tools and knowledge to help dispel the shame that often surrounds these topics.

Within the church, Crystal has worked in various capacities including youth and adult ministry, church administrative boards at the local and national level, women's ministry, as well as teaching and pastoring. In her spare time, Crystal loves building with Legos and traveling with her son. She currently leads a Bible study and prayer group in her home in Arlington, VA.

Chapter 8
The Woman's Enemy

Now the serpent was more subtil than any beast of the field which the Lord God had made. And he said unto the woman, yea, hath God said, Ye shall not eat of every tree of the garden?
—*Genesis 3:1*

Eve knew that she was a majestic ruler. She had dominion alongside her husband Adam. Her queendom was unchallenged. She didn't think about the prospect of an enemy lurking within her territory. However, it was clear that after taking a bite from the fruit, everything had changed. Eve and her husband immediately knew good and evil. They felt the effects of shame. They decided to hide themselves.

Why did she risk it all? How did she even get to this place? Physically, she was still in her home. Things were technically the same on the outside, but as she looked around Eve knew she had entered a whole new dimension of reality. A reality that didn't look or feel like anything she knew before.

It was then that she realized what God really meant. He told her so much. She spent countless moments with Him, basking in the glory of the garden. God the Father showered her with love and adoration. Before this moment, she was unashamed of her perfect skin, her hair and body. But now she realized she needed to be covered. She could hear God's movement in the garden. A look in her husband's direction, and she saw he was just as terrified and confused about their future as she was.

There were honestly no words that could capture the new negative emotions she was experiencing all at once. She felt helpless, she was afraid, anxious and felt completely exposed. As she heard the judgements of God, she could not fully comprehend their meaning. There was so much shock from the experience of their eyes being opened and adjusting to this new nightmare that was now real. As God spoke, I believe she felt the power and strength of each judgement just as He spoke it. Eve wept bitterly.

Lucifer was an enemy of God, and automatically became an enemy of Eve. He is described as an adversary (see 1 Peter 5:8). I believe before the fall, God taught Adam and Eve kingdom principles. They were made in His image and were told to rule and have dominion over the garden. Part of Eve's dominion training incorporated her understanding of who she was and what she was tasked to do. God had many conversations with Eve about her queendom and position. These conversations were now just tender memories of a world lost.

A key lesson that we can learn from Eve is that the extent of a person's dominion is not visible to the naked eye. It does not only encompass the garden that you can see, or the people who are in your inner circle. You have jurisdiction and authority which transcends this physical world. Eve did not realize her own enemy was within her jurisdiction. The one who wanted her power was a familiar face but clearly a different spirit. I believe this is why it is written in 1 John 4:1 for us not to believe every spirit, but to test the spirit to discern their spiritual alignment.

From Genesis chapter 3 we can see that not only was the enemy searching for ways to steal dominion, but also to establish systems to perpetuate a chaotic environment. This is why angels were placed to guard the tree of eternal life, to protect humanity from living forever separated due to sin.

A closer look at Eve's story teaches us queendom threats can be internal and external. External threats are the threats outside of us. These threats try to invoke an emotional reaction. Eve was truly different from Adam not only physically, but emotionally as well. One of my friends calls this attribute of women our emotional power. A true gift and part of our queendom arsenal.

A lesson to be learned is don't be afraid to confront external threats and bullies in the midst of your garden. Protect your emotions and remember it is you who has the power over them. The devil's level of authority and rulership is only an illusion. He has no authority or rulership in this earth by his own might. Our enemy has to influence others in order to manifest his kingdom in the earth the same way he influenced and manipulated the snake.

Some internal threats are described in the Bible. These are characteristics, actions and attitudes that have roots inside the soul and flesh parts of us.

Now the works of the flesh are manifest, which are these; adultery, fornication, uncleanness, lasciviousness, idolatry, witchcraft, hatred, variance, emulations, wrath, strife, seditions, heresies, envyings, murders, drunkenness, revelings, and such like: of the which I tell you before, as I have also told you in time past, that they which do such things shall not inherit the kingdom of God.

— Galatians 5:19-21

It is interesting to note the next portion of scripture references the fruit we should have. But the fruit of the Spirit is love, joy, peace, longsuffering, gentleness, goodness, faith, meekness, temperance: against such there is no law. One translation even closes with saying, "Never set a law for these qualities, for they are meant to be limitless." Similar to how life originally was in the garden, the fruit outside the forbidden zone had no law or limit assigned to them.

I believe the enemy is always trying to attack our minds and beliefs. We all have gone through the Eve experience, places in our lives where we thought we were less than what God has called us to be. One of the lies the enemy used while tempting Eve was that God was holding back from her. The fruit would make her "like god." Isn't it ironic how Satan's fall was for that very reason?

Maybe, like Eve, for a while we have walked with God. We have a relationship and timed conversations where we meet, and think we understand and know Him, yet we fall from grace. She may have spent many cool evenings with God in the garden. But did she know she was talking to a devil? How many times has she done this? What other avenues were used to plant seeds of doubt?

Be vigilant, be wise, and be aware. A good exercise I do often is to pray over my relationships and conversations. Know your enemy from the inside out. Study your Word, understand your weaknesses. Be honest with where you are now and where your queendom stands. Periodically assess your level of leadership and influence. Evaluate your heart and ask God to reveal hidden things that need to be corrected. Ladies, we were *Fashioned by God to Rule the World.* Let us rule with the authority and leadership model He has provided in His Word, as well as spoken to our hearts.

Fashioned by God to Rule the World

Journal

Journal

Chapter 9
The PowHER of Focus: Overcoming Distractions

Saneeta Golden. MHS, MSW

Saneeta's HERstory

My name is Saneeta Golden, and I am a successful serial entrepreneur and passionate life coach. I began my life coaching business at the beginning of 2019, and it took off quickly. My main coaching business is called "Unlock Your Power™"; it is designed to help women become more self-aware and authentic while pushing them to take massive actions in their lives.

I've always wanted to become an entrepreneur. I didn't grow up with a silver spoon in my mouth and I was never taught to have or know how to establish a successful business. A lot of what I have today is thanks to my tenacity and desire to learn.

I have always wanted more for myself and my children. I wanted to be someone that instills the importance of loving yourself and being true to yourself. Thanks to my knowledge and persistence, I am privileged to have a constant flow of clients whose lives I have helped to change by unlocking their true power.

Hearing their touching testimonies and seeing their success is nothing short of amazing! Although they have endured many trials and tribulations, they still have managed to remove themselves from the obstacles that they had to face.

Everyone has to go through some adversities to grow. But don't ever let your pain hold you back from being the best version of yourself. Never allow it to take control of you and distract you from your focus. I am the perfect example of this. I am currently dealing with health issues that came as a huge surprise. All of this time, I've been very healthy. I've always tried my best to eat well and exercise to keep myself fit.

However, in December 2020 I was diagnosed with a Thymoma tumor. And it shook me to my very foundation. Initially, even the doctors didn't believe it was cancerous because, on the surface, it didn't appear to be the case. This was a rare condition. It wasn't until my arm began hurting severely that they did an x-ray that revealed tumors in my chest. It was a tough time for me, although I've been through a lot of uncertainty throughout my life. This time, I think I was just plain scared of going through all of the tedious tests and scans.

Later, I was told that I needed to undergo chemotherapy before I could get the tumor removed via surgery. I remember vividly how I was sobbing and feeling frightened for myself, my family, and especially for my precious girls and husband. I thought, *what will I do? What can I not do? How will I feel?* I was confused as question after question of uncertainty hit me like relentless waves at the sea. I wondered, *why me? Why was this my trial?* Soon after, I was faced with days of being depressed and worried.

It was at my most dire moments that I realized I was not alone. The Lord was there with me all the while. God did not give me the spirit of fear. But instead, He gave me the spirit of power, love, and a sound mind! I knew deep inside that I can do anything through Christ who strengthens me. After that, it felt as if every scripture that I knew returned to me. I felt as if I was being healed internally by the stripes of Jesus. And at least had my lovely praying mother who is always there for me. My prayer life increased and my faith grew by the day.

It's still difficult, but I keep waking up to see a new day and I count them all as my blessings. Every day is not always easy—I've now completed my fourth treatment. Each one is harder, and the side effects are difficult, however, I am blessed to tell the story and encourage someone else to continue to have faith.

Losing my hair, weight, and ability to eat at times, I continue to fight and teach my "unlock my power" principles, while undergoing this process. The shock of the diagnosis made me realize that no matter how healthy you believe you are, never ignore pain. Always seek medical attention for new occurrences.

Right now, I am bravely waiting for my surgery. I am still focused because I will never let something like this distract me from who I want to be. I exercise, eat, and do things I love as a mother and a wife. I am grateful and I know inside my mind that I have already won. My focus is true to my aim and I will not divert from my path, no matter what!

All of this has made me incredibly grateful for what I have accomplished, and I am still striving every day to do more. Watching the flowers blossom from all my watering and care is surreal. I am blessed by God to be able to live such a fulfilled life.

I've now shared a portion of my story with you, but this isn't about me. It's about how I can help you reach your destination with the help of the Almighty. This is my special message to you.

"No matter who you are, or where you are from, no matter what your next chapter entails, embrace it boldly! Time passes by, people will come and go, but your belief in yourself and your dreams must never die."

You need to always remind yourself that you deserve the next level of success. Believe it or not, your past, good or bad, has prepared and qualified you. This is how I try to think when adversities hit, because they will. The Lord has prepared me for my journey and He always provides me a way to learn my lessons so I can improve and do better. With that, I would like to tell you how I look at things when it comes to focus and distractions.

Chapter 9
The PowHER of Focus: Overcoming Distractions

For GOD doth know that in that day ye eat thereof, then your eyes shall be opened, and ye shall be as gods, knowing good and evil.
And when the woman saw that the tree was good for food and that it was pleasant to the eyes, and a tree to be desired to make one wise, she took off the fruit thereof, and did eat, and gave also unto her husband with her: and he did eat.
—Genesis 3:5-6

This part of the Bible has always left a huge impression on me. It taught me that if we don't stay focused and trust in the Word of the Lord, we can easily become distracted. This can change the direction of our life, and delay our chance for success.

You see, Adam and Eve ate the fruit from the tree inside of the Garden of Eden thanks to temptation from the devil. She ate from the one thing that was forbidden instead of being thankful for all of the things that she was already provided. The negative focus clouded her mind. She succumbed to temptation because she was distracted and became curious about what the devil said.

When you get distracted with what you don't have or with situations that other people may enjoy, your mind becomes confused. You begin to take life for granted. You forget the salvation, the sunshine, the flowers, and countless other gifts that the Lord has already provided for you. For me, overcoming distractions can only happen when you have a deep sense of gratitude and when you allow the light of the Lord's presence to pour into you. Focus on what you want, reach out your hand as far as you can, and the Lord will meet you.

Fashioned by God to Rule the World
Your PowHer, Focus and Discipline

If you've ever had trouble starting something or struggled to finish something that you started, you are not alone. Every person that I know, at one time or another inevitably has experienced this. Yes, humans can be quite incapable of concentrating on a specific goal or task. Thanks to the distractions offered by our desires and emotions, we do a poor job of figuring out the correct course of action to take. We can even be given a recipe for success and still get off track from following it. So, how can a person tell if they have a problem focusing?

Here's what I tell my coaching clients all of the time. If you have tasks or projects that you have not finished, have lost interest in or simply did not follow through on, then you have a lack of focus. When you constantly experience this, you will start feeling like a failure. It will feel as if you are unable to accomplish anything meaningful in your life. But that's far from the truth! If you just learn to focus properly, you'll gain the ability to become wildly successful at anything you wish to do. It is a skill you can learn, and I've seen this happen many times with my clients.

Keys to Creating More Focus in Your Life

"Quitters never win, and winners never quit!" For me, this phrase perfectly sums up the meaning of the word *tenacity*. Creating and keeping a strong focus is hard work and you need to keep improving on it every single day. However, it is a skill that can serve you for the rest of your life, if you make the effort to attain it. Believe in yourself and you'll be able to gain the ability to help you succeed at whatever you set out to do.

Your commitment to your vision and the process is essential. Without commitment, you'll find it hard to focus and get motivated to keep yourself going. Hence, always make sure that you really want that goal that you've set. If it's not something that you really want and it's just something that other people have, then you may need to rethink your goals. Having a "half-hearted" goal means that you'll never be able to commit to it in the first place. The second a shiny, new distraction comes along you will bail.

Start setting achievable, measurable, and realistic goals for yourself. Take baby steps. As you achieve small wins along your journey, you'll feel inspired to take the next step. They say that your attitude determines your altitude. I couldn't agree more. With positivity, nothing is ever too hard, hopeless, a waste of time, or too big of a challenge. That's how those who are successful don't ever seem to give up when they encounter setbacks. They get right back up and move on.

Because being able to focus takes a tremendous amount of self-discipline, you need to be strong mentally to stick to your plans. Always track your progress and change whenever necessary. Dedicate yourself to your commitments and avoid any temptations, self-doubt, and negative thoughts while still being flexible in case the unexpected happens.

The next thing you need to avoid is procrastination. To me, procrastination is akin to a thief who is out to steal your results. If you tend to hesitate and overthink things before doing them, stop! You are not doing yourself any favors by stalling, and you are actually setting yourself up to fail.

To be successful, another important key is to be enthusiastic. Without enthusiasm, you will quickly lose interest in your journey. Always remember how you felt when you first set your vision. That very same enthusiasm needs to be kept to maintain your momentum to tackle the tough road ahead. As time progresses, we naturally lose this momentum. That's when you need to get yourself excited, once again, and recommit yourself. It's like re-fueling that car after a long drive. To do this, positive self-talk can work wonders for you.

I am big on being consistent. I truly believe that consistency is crucial to our focus. That's why I spend at least thirty minutes to an hour a day, or more, on my action steps to bring my vision closer to fruition. To some, thirty minutes or an hour may seem insignificant but for those with an already busy life (like me) it's a Godsend!

Overcome Distractions and Become More Focused, for Good!

Every day, we experience unending noise around us. Most of this serves as a distraction to your goals. Think about the time you spend scrolling endlessly on your social media platforms. It's no wonder that we can hardly get anything done these days. That's why we need to be selective. We need to learn how to turn away and sacrifice some of the things we are doing now, to reduce the number of distractions. So, how can we get rid of distractions? By employing self-discipline. If you are disciplined in your work and your goals, you will undoubtedly be able to accomplish everything that you want to achieve. It's not easy to be self-disciplined, but the good news is the rewards are going to be worth it.

There are many areas inside of our lives where we should become disciplined. For starters, we should be disciplined with our thoughts. Do not let your fears carry you away; fear and worry block productive solutions. That's why we need to learn to be disciplined enough so that any time our inner worries appear, we need to stop them immediately.

Next, we need self-discipline with the words that come out of our mouths. We shouldn't want to say anything negative. If you have an impulse to say something negative, close your mouth. Even when you accidentally blurt out something negative, cut it mid-sentence and say no more. Correct it instantly and change your next words into something positive. Always be self-disciplined to evaluate yourself during your conversations.

Being disciplined with our actions is very important, too. We need to do whatever is necessary now, and not put important tasks off because they may never get done. That's why I always advise my clients to write down their goals and check them off one by one. What gets written down gets done! Don't be led off track by someone who is undisciplined.

From my experience, most people desire to accomplish something great. However, when it comes down to the hard work, they start to hesitate because they fear what all is involved. Exercising, learning, planning, writing, phoning, and pushing through even when there seems to be no light at the end of the tunnel, is crucial. Yes, self-discipline means doing necessary things like exercising even when you do not feel like it. Write that book that you've always wanted to, even when you don't see where the work will take you. Work diligently on your project even if it is uncertain whether or not you will succeed.

It can get really hard, but we've got to put in the work and leave the results and outcomes to the Lord. If we give it our all, then we'd have no regrets. At the very least, we'll learn something from it. Being focused means putting yourself out there, day after day, even when you are tired. It means keeping yourself fired up when there's no one else there to encourage you. It means taking the time and energy to be masterful at something new. It means taking the required steps to transform your life for the better. You keep doing it tirelessly, never giving up, until one day you can say you have arrived.

But that's not all there is to it. Being disciplined should be all-encompassing in all areas of our lives. Here's a true story. I used to have a few clients who were super-focused when it came to working out. They would run regardless of the weather and then they would hit the gym for at least two hours every day, no matter what.

However, these are the same clients who were unable to focus on their side hustles. They would get distracted easily and hang out with their friends or binge-watch movies on Netflix. They also got easily hooked on their social media feeds and found themselves scrolling mindlessly, wasting time.

Because of this they felt terribly guilty and unproductive. If only their discipline was not limited to only certain areas of their lives. When I pointed this out to them, they made strides in their careers by channeling that same focused energy from their workouts into other parts of their lives.

Now, the hard part when it comes to discipline is that change does not usually happen overnight. This is especially true if you are coming from a lower place emotionally, financially, and spiritually.

For example, if you wish to have money for the down payment of a new house, you simply cannot keep charging your credit cards all of the time. You've got to be disciplined with a saving strategy and not spending unnecessarily until you turn your dreams into reality. If you dream of being creative, like a painter or a writer, but you have no clue about these subjects, you've got to be disciplined and get focused on learning and perfecting your craft. You've got to do whatever it takes to bring you closer to your goals. Don't let distractions stop you from progressing.

Here's a quick tip. When you are learning something new, be disciplined to be non-judgmental. Don't start condemning your own efforts. Don't let other people's opinions distract you from excellence. Encourage yourself and visualize yourself winning in your new profession. Enjoy the process and keep practicing and improving until one day the world will no longer ignore your existence.

One of the biggest factors toward success and mastery is time. The amount of time you spend on your craft will largely determine your skills. That's why, when you discipline yourself to work on your skills for just thirty minutes a day, you will see results in the long run. Imagine polishing your abilities for just half an hour a day, for ten years. That thirty-minute, undistracted focus, will turn into something powerful. Turn off that TV for an hour, and all of a sudden, you've gained an hour that you can use to work on your goals. Your success will be determined by what you do with your extra time.

Unleashing Your True Potential: 10 Tips to Improve Your Focus

1. *Learn to Analyze Your Current Situation*
If you've been having a hard time finding the success and peace that you want in life, you need to learn to be more self-disciplined. To start, you need to have a certain amount of clarity about your own situation. Get a clear picture of all of the things that are helping you to get closer to your goals and find out what's distracting or hindering you from your true potential. Write them down and make the necessary changes needed to change your course.

2. *Set a Strong Main Goal*
When you are clear about what you want in life and who you wish to become, you can set a strong goal. This goal needs to be big, and to achieve it you need to be able to focus and attain a great deal of self-discipline. Learn to visualize the biggest aspects of your life and identify the part of you that needs to be changed. Then set that as one of your primary goals.

3. *List Your Smaller Goals*
No matter how grand your primary goal is, you will not be able to attain it without first taking several steps. Yes, it is a journey, and for that we need to set smaller, achievable, short-term goals. Take weight loss for an example, if you wish to get rid of a certain amount of fat around your waist, you simply cannot reach your "perfect weight" without smaller goals like eating healthy, starting a consistent exercise regime, or being disciplined when shopping at your local mart.

Set those small achievable goals, take one step at a time, keep at it and soon you will see the fruits of your labor manifesting into reality.

4. *Set Realistic Goals*

Whatever your goals are, make sure they are realistic and achievable. That's why I always tell my clients to set SMART goals. Remember, take baby steps. For example, maybe you are looking to lose thirty pounds. Start with an initial five pounds. Or maybe you want to be able to run fifty miles. Start by going for that one mile run in the first few months, and then gradually step it up as your body grows stronger. If you've only got one hour to spare per day, then try to set your goals aligned to that amount of time.

Break down that seemingly impossible task into small digestible and realistic goals and you'll do just fine. It doesn't matter how long it takes, there's no rush. Focus and you'll get there.

5. *Plan Five Steps Ahead*

Whatever you set out to do, you're likely to be met with problems. But don't be dismayed. You can plan ahead and anticipate issues. Often, these problems are a result of your own actions. Make sure you are disciplined at all times, and keep your eyes on the prize. Don't quit if it gets hard, and if you anticipate the problems, you'll be able to overcome them. When there is a will, there is a way!

6. *Learn to Track Your Progress*

Know that when you begin to reach some of your goals, that will not be the end of it. To know if you are really becoming more self-disciplined, you should track your progress with a simple chart. One method that I recommend my clients do is to ask someone close to them to help them with the tracking. That way, there's someone unbiased who is holding you accountable.

This is crucial because when you create these milestones, you need to be able to have mini celebrations as you meet them. These small wins will keep you focused and excited to achieve more.

7. *Sometimes, a Little Force Can't Hurt*
I am going to say this without mincing words. Improving your self-discipline for a specific goal is hard. That's why sometimes it becomes imperative that you force yourself to do the things that you don't like or are uncomfortable with. Focus on the results and just do it! Remember, be willing to do whatever it takes.

8. *Inspiring Others Can Have a Positive Effect on You*
It's no secret that a lot of people have difficulty when it comes to their own discipline. Now that you've learned some of my methods to get more self-disciplined and improve dramatically, try helping others do the same. When you are shining like a star, others around you will get that spark of inspiration from you. It'll boost their confidence and you'll be able to enforce your own motivation.

9. *Identifying the Roots of the Problems*
On your path towards total focus, you will be met with difficulties. To improve, you need to eliminate all of the bad habits that may arise. So, identify the root of your problems and fix them. You'll find it to be the most effective way to improve your focus and remove yourself from any distractions that will affect your goals in a negative way.

For example, if you want to excel at work and arrive earlier every morning to make a better impression, you will have to start waking up early. You may have to cut down on those late-night TV binges or stop mindlessly browsing on social media.

10. *Follow and Commit 100% to Your Plan*
Plan what you want to achieve carefully. Map a path and carry out that plan. While everything might not always go as expected, remember that this too shall pass. Don't get frustrated. Anticipate it. Pick yourself up, recover quickly and forgive yourself. Continue on your path. Believe in the powHer of focus and let the Lord take over. Before long, you will see the success that you've always wanted.

My Final Advice

Through my years of struggle, pain, and finally success, my biggest takeaway is that I realized that the Lord will not put you through a trial without giving you peace. He will never forsake you. Be grateful in spite of the situation and keep trusting the Lord. You become what your mind thinks, and what you say. So, speak life over yourself. Speak healing and declare all of the things that you wish to transform.

I want to see everyone do well and live a purpose-driven life. I often find myself boldly declaring that we are all valuable and intelligent. What we do with our knowledge is completely up to us. If you are feeling doubts about your future, heed these words of encouragement.

"Now is not the time to be afraid. Now is not the time to doubt. Nor is it the time to question your place. The truth is that you are more ready than you realize. Just go with the flow and the Lord will protect you. Have faith and believe. Focus on your path and destroy all distractions!"

Fashioned by God to Rule the World

Journal

Fashioned by God to Rule the World

Journal

Chapter 10
Eve: First Lady of the Universe

Kim W. Miller, B.S.

Kim's HERstory

Kim W. Miller aka "Lady K" was born and raised in Chicago, IL as the eldest in her family. She showed the potential to become a leader at an early age, discovering her desire to write. The first piece that she wrote was a poem entitled "Day Break" at the age of eleven. Kim's mom was influential in her being baptized and becoming part of the body of Christ at the age of thirteen. She attended both Richards Vocational and Jones Commercial High Schools. After graduation, she attended Chicago College of Commerce for Court Reporting. Marriage was quickly on the horizon; a year later she was married to Glenn E. Miller.

Shortly thereafter, her husband was called into the evangelistic ministry, in which he remained for twelve years. He was later called to pastor BCOM Ministries, now Life Christian Center International, in Bellwood, IL. From the start of the church ministry, the growth increased each year, and the church purchased several properties, including the church building, a two-story administrative building with the BCOM Learning Center on the first floor, and a youth center called the "Shack."

Kim has served as a pastor's wife for thirty years, she is the mother of four adult children—Jenese, Veronica, Glenn II (Andrea), and Jeremiah (Beatrice), and two grandsons, Noah James and Nico Lewis.

Kim returned to college to receive her associate and Bachelor of Science degrees in small business management with a focus on entrepreneurship from the University of Phoenix. She has several areas of interest including beauty. She is an independent beauty consultant for Mary Kay. A second area of interest involves her love for jewelry. In 2020, Kim initiated the launch of a dream and Kjv Exquisites Legacy Jewelry was born. Named for her and her daughters, Kjv stands for Kim, Jenese and Veronica.

In ministry, she is the Women of Valor director, one of the Associate Pastors and assistant to the Pastor, executive board member, operations manager, worship leader, speaker and teacher at Life Christian Center International. She is also one of the teaching pastors and North America global director of the Women of Vision and Destiny Ministries Worldwide.

Chapter 10
Eve: First Lady of the Universe

And Adam called his wife's name Eve; because she was the mother of all living.
—*Genesis 3:20*

In the beginning, God! He who is the beginner of all things created the heavens and the earth, illuminated it with light and filled it with His spoken Word, and His matchless, extravagant handiwork. God was in no rush when He began the revealing and manifestation of His master plan for this place called earth. It's amazing to see in the pages of His Word how methodical He was in the beginning. He left nothing to chance. Everything He called into existence was on purpose and for a purpose. Earth was completely designed for the habitation of all living creatures. What He created was in operational order from the moment He spoke, "Let there be…"

After creating the earth and placing the fowls in the air, fish in the seas, the cattle and creeping things, tree-yielding fruit, herb- yielding seed after its kind, God saw it was good. Even though there was no one on earth as of yet to manage or till the ground, God, who is infinite in wisdom, caused a mist to come up from the earth to water the whole face of the ground.

Now, this is all so amazing and wonderous to contemplate and consider—nothing was here before God spoke it into existence. The magnificent God of the universe simply uttered words, and it all came to be. But He wasn't finished. There were living creatures on the earth without an authoritarian to govern and rule over them; therefore, God spoke again. Genesis 1:26 says, "And God said, let us make man in our image, after our likeness and let them have dominion over the fish of the sea, and over the fowl of the air, and over the cattle, and over all the earth and over every creeping thing that creepeth upon the earth."

Here's what I envisioned from this scripture. First, God said let us make man in our image, after our likeness. God thought this thing out and was organized and structured with an end goal in mind. When He said make *man*, He knew the inward and outward function of what He wanted man to be, look like and the emotions he was to have. Every bone, vein, blood cell, and internal organ was in its proper place and accounted for. God never had to go back to the drawing board to try and fix any part of man due to lack of functionality.

Just think about it, man was etched onto the blueprint of God's thoughts with Him knowing every intricate part of this being, and how his body would operate. He designed the smallest details to the largest organ of the body. He executed what the blueprint called for man to be. Man was made in the image and likeness of God, possessing a moral likeness—sinless, holy and having a heart to fellowship with God in moral obedience. He had the ability to have intimate communion with God.

Second, He said *them*—man and woman will have dominion over the fish, fowls, cattle and all creeping things on the earth. The man nor woman hadn't even been brought into physical existence yet, but God declared what was to be before it existed. God was showing us from the beginning what spiritual altitude we should reign in and occupy. God's statement at this point is futuristic. The Bible says that God knows our end from our beginning. He sees our entire life backwards!

God's order is impeccably outstanding and cannot be compared to anything we could plan, put together or orchestrate. Our thoughts and plans couldn't stand next to what God has organized and created. When we make plans, organize and re-organize, there are times that something that should have been included in the plan is left out. When it comes to God, His timing is precise, His organization is unimaginable, and nothing is missed. It is complete and it is finished. He can pace Himself, and never has to rush because He's not governed by our limits of time.

All of creation in the earth and the element of habitation is complete. God now moves to the next phase of His masterful blueprint. The creation of man. Just thinking of man being formed from the dust of the earth is mind-boggling and has provoked numerous conversations from all types of scientists and scholars. Many evolutionists have developed their theories of how humanity started. This is the question that remains for many: how can we, as human beings, exist in a body made of dust? It just seems unbelievable, right?

Well, God is sovereign. Sovereign means that He possesses supreme or ultimate power, and He can do as He pleases whether we understand it or not. The Almighty God did it, it is so, and I believe it just as He said in His Word. Now let's look more closely at how God brought man into existence. Genesis 2:7 says, "And the Lord God formed man of the dust of the ground and breathed into his nostrils the breath of life and man became a living soul."

When we take an in depth look at the physique of man, it is amazing to fathom how all of the intricate details were thought about, let alone linked together to work in their capacity. It is amazing how the Scripture reveals to us that we are His workmanship, and fearfully and wonderfully made. But, just as God spoke the other workings of creation into existence, He did the same for the formation of man, and with one breath He brought forth a living soul and the beginning of humanity.

What I have learned about God—and am still learning—is when He starts a thing, He knows how the completed picture will look and the steps to that point of completion. Adam was created and given instructions about the trees in the garden—which ones could be touched for eating, and which one was forbidden for eating. He was also given the consequences of indulging in the forbidden Tree of Knowledge of Good and Evil.

I believe Adam had an open, intimate relationship with God, so it was very clear to him what he could and couldn't do. Out of all the creatures on the earth, there was no one of Adam's caliber. During the time God and Adam spent together, God saw Adam didn't have a compatible mate. God's frame of measuring time is very different than ours. The proclamation of God's timing is found in 2 Peter 3:8, "But, beloved, be not ignorant of this one thing, that one day is with the Lord as a thousand years, and a thousand years as one day."

With that, I believe God saw in that span of time He and Adam had fellowship with each other, that Adam had no one of his kind with which to form a relationship or create a line of communication. God would have observed Adam and that he was alone, with no one of the same mental caliber or same level. You see, all of creation prior to Adam had a mate and another creature after their kind. This gave all the created beings an avenue of reproducing and the ability to continue life.

The only living creation without a partner was Adam. Genesis is all about "beginnings" and "firsts." So, God spoke again and said, "It is not good that the man should be alone; I will make, or fashion, him a help meet for him" (Genesis 2:18). This is where Adam's help meet came onto the scene. God caused a deep sleep to fall upon Adam. It was the first operation with anesthesia-like affects. Adam didn't awaken until the work was completed.

What God chose to take from Adam and place in his help meet was a rib. The rib, or rib cage, is vital in the human body. The rib cage surrounds the lungs and heart and serves as an important means of protection for the vital organs. This rib symbolized the bone which would equalize the man and woman. I see the rib being taken from the man's side—at his level not from his back or lower half of him. The rib is makes them equal or side by side. They now are one in the same.

This action is fulfilled and takes us back to Genesis 1:26, *"And God said, let us make man in our image, after our likeness: and let them have dominion over the fish of the sea, and over the cattle, and over all the earth, and over every creeping thing that creepeth upon the earth.* Man and woman were the "them" referred to in the scripture. They were not separate, but one in the same, created equal. This is absolutely amazing. It was God's intention in the beginning for mankind. We were *Fashioned by God (Himself) to Rule the World*!

When Adam awoke from his surgery, God brought the woman to the man. Adam was enthralled by what he saw in the other human now standing before him. The twenty-third verse of Genesis expresses his emotions: "And Adam said, this is now bone of my bones, and flesh of my flesh; she shall be called Woman, because she was taken out of Man." I believe he was absolutely drawn to his wife. He was to cleave to her and be one flesh. Woman is her name. She was taken out of man and created to fulfill or help meet his obligations and goals.

I always thought the term was helpmate, not helpmeet. But there's a big difference. The word that is translated helpmeet in Hebrew is *ezer* and *kenegdo*. Ezer is described multiple times as God being a helper to Israel and a couple of times as being allies of Israel's in battle. This meaning shows God as helper, defender, sword and shield. Using it in this context seems to exemplify woman (or helpmeet) as a warrior. Kenegdo, means "as in front of him," or, of the same nature or mirrored. This translation of helpmeet shows what a sinless relationship between a man and woman looks like—a true partnership.

So, her name was woman and from the looks of things she is really Adam—she was taken from him and is the intimate part of him bone of his bone and flesh of his flesh. My eyes were opened when I pulled this reference. Look at how far God's thoughts are from our thoughts, even regarding His creation of man and woman. "Then both Eve and her husband are called "Adam." "Male and female created he them ... and called their name Adam" (Genesis 5:2).

According to *All the Women of the Bible*, "this inclusive name—Adam—implies that the divine ideal for man and wife is not merely that of association but an indissoluble unity." How amazing is our God? When He created them, He gave them one name—Adam. Eve is the name given after the fall. Eve means "life" or "life-giving," or "mother of all who have life," and her life is in us all.

I believe the enemy, Satan, had a mission to disrupt and pervert everything God had set in motion. We all know he wanted to be like the Most High and take His place. In him making a move on God so to speak, he was banished, fell like lighting from heaven and his place of authority was stripped from him. Of course, he will not be ecstatic about what God was doing now. So why not destroy the "first" Adam and bring death to a nation who had endless life flowing through them. What I'm grateful for is the Sovereign, Omniscient God who had a master plan already scripted.

I often wondered, and still do, why didn't the man protect the woman from making a bad decision when the tempter came along? Especially since they were so connected. She was deceived and he went right along with her. I think that might be a question for God when we all get to heaven.

There are a number of things to explore regarding Eve. She was unique and a distinct woman. Eve wasn't born, but made from the rib of her husband, Adam. Therefore, she had no earthly mother or father. She was the first of her kind—fashioned by God—a design original. She couldn't look back through her bloodline to see who she favored or who she got her personality from. She had no lineage to speak of, or to discover, as we do now.

We have the capability of finding our ancestors through various search engines, tracing our roots as far back as it will take us. Eve was the first woman to ever exist on earth so the only trace for her was back to her Creator, God. She had no instructions or "how to" books for anything she was about to encounter within her new life after the fall. There was nothing to teach her how to cook, clean, or raise children, let alone care for a husband and herself. It was learn as you go, on the job training.

Fashioned by God to Rule the World

In reading one of Dr. Cindy Trimm's books, I came across a statement that stood out to me, "When you are the first in anything, there is no guide for you to follow. Whether it be the first woman VP, firstborn in a family, first to break glass ceilings, first lady of a newly founded church and so on. You become the trailblazer." That's what Eve became, a trailblazer.

It is ironic that I was chosen to write this chapter. The reason I say that is because I fall into the "first" category in so areas in my life. I am the firstborn child to my mother. Being the first born afforded me some advantages, but also some disadvantages. When you are the first, you do become a trailblazer. This is your lot without you even knowing it. Being first causes you to create systems for how things operate, even within the dynamics of a family.

There is no dictionary or guidebook pointing you in the right direction of how to walk, talk, eat—none of the beginning phase wonders. At least the second child has the opportunity to watch the older one to mimic what they see them do, but not that first child. They are what we call the "guinea pig." The parents, most of the time, are learning in their life of parenthood, just as that child is learning through their new adventures of childhood.

Generally, the first child becomes a leader, I believe by default. There are cases where there are differences. I remember taking charge as being the oldest. Whenever we went places, I was always looking after my sister and little did I know, I would become her role model. It just became my natural instinct to take care of my sister—making sure she had what I had and so on. That was, until I got tired of my mini-me following along. I am also, the first lady to my pastor and husband, and my church family at Life Christian Center International.

I remember disliking that title. I didn't want anyone to call me first lady or "first" as I've heard some say. I'm not totally sure why. Maybe it was an identity issue. I wonder, did I really see myself as the first lady or was I just not recognizing the office I was operating within? I always thought Lord, I didn't have the opportunity to glean from those first ladies I admired during my teen years, nor was I tutored by them as I desired once in this position. That opportunity would have been given in a perfect world.

Since we were founders—not having an established church appointed to us—we were being initiated into the "first" club. I remember that initial Sunday in May 1991, the doors of Bethel Community Outreach Ministries (BCOM) opened. So many emotions flooded my brain, heart and soul at the time. I was scared of the unknown, to say the least. What were we doing? We needed God's hand upon us. Back then, we knew nothing of being trained to step into this role that was going to mold our lives forever.

With God's guidance, we started with six people, increased our family, maintained faith throughout this new life of adventure—through us growing up spiritually and encountering all sorts of trials and temptations. The enemy would have loved to have create pitfalls, yet through it all we are here today, thirty years later. So, I believe I can relate with Eve being the first of her kind to be on this earth blazing the trail for us women who would be the first to blaze our own trails in "first" experiences.

If we look in Genesis 3, we see how the woman was beguiled by the serpent. The Hebrew word for beguiled is *nasha* meaning to mentally delude and morally seduce. The serpent imposed his misleading belief upon the woman through the seduction of authority and power—being like God. Have you ever been put in a situation where you were totally vulnerable, the wool was pulled over your eyes and you had to make decisions within minutes? You made decisions not knowing the intent of the other party. You may have made the wrong choice later to find out that you had been placed in a trap of deception. You unknowingly were being deceived and fooled.

Ever been there? I have. It's only by the grace of God that I was not consumed. In my case, I was shaken by the Lord God. I was given instructions on what to do while even being in a vulnerable state, and the hidden pathway was revealed through the illumination that came from His Word. God's Word was my way out!

This attack of Satan was ultimately done to throw a monkey wrench into God's plan through the defilement of humanity. Satan wanted the very man God created and the woman He fashioned in His image and likeness to be in a fallen state—a state he'd also brought upon himself. Since Satan couldn't directly overthrow God and sit on His throne, he went on an indirect attack of God's created human beings. Remember, Lucifer coveted God's authority and power. Here is the great reveal of why Satan entered the full-blown attack of deception on the woman, Eve.

The Word says, "How you are fallen from heaven, O Lucifer son of the morning! How you are cut down to the ground, you who weakened the nations! For you have said in your heart: 'I will ascend into heaven, I will exalt my throne above the stars of God; I will also sit on the mount of the congregation on the farthest sides of the north; I will ascend above the heights of the clouds, I will be like the Most High" (Isaiah 14:12-14).

This encounter was one of Eve's "firsts." She didn't quite know how to handle meeting her rival. Wait, she didn't even know she had a rival. She didn't realize there was another creature out there competing with her authority. God had already given Adam and his wife the authority to rule and dominate (Genesis 1:26). You see, the serpent knew he had been banished from his position due to his evil desire to be just like God. With no example to follow, she did what she thought was best. Her thought was to take the fruit from tree and eat, and give to her husband.

After both had taken and eaten, their eyes were opened. They immediately realized and grasped what it felt like to be disconnected from God. Their intimacy with God was now broken and they were about to become acquainted with death.

One thing I love about God though, is He always has a plan and a way of escape already prepared.

With God fashioning the woman, my mind races to the scripture, "I will praise thee; for I am fearfully and wonderfully made marvelous are thy works; and that my soul knoweth right well (Psalm 139:14). Eve was skillfully shaped, crafted and fitted for man. God's hand glided over her, molded every part of her in the fullness of His beauty and grace. God not only made her to perfection in body, but also in mind. What she was to become was lodged into God's thoughts and those thoughts illuminated the express image of Eve, the first lady.

Once Adam and Eve's eyes were opened, they saw their nakedness and were ashamed. The woman now became the first dressmaker. She immediately uses her creativity, given to her by God, to cover both her and her husband: "they sewed fig leaves together and made themselves aprons," (Genesis 3:7 NIV). Remember in Genesis 2, they were naked and not ashamed. But right as we enter the next chapter, they were naked and ashamed. The first represents their sinless state with the second representing their state of sin and death.

I've often thought to myself, how is it that they knew what to do? Creating an apron to cover themselves? God made them in His likeness; therefore, designing was an innate part of them. When they ate the fruit from the tree of knowledge of good and evil, they instantly had knowledge and creativity. Those of us who are creative can see things in our minds before they materialize—that's what a designer does. They blaze the trail creating the path for others to follow. I believe that is what the woman did.

I had the opportunity to watch a special on CNN of some of the most outstanding FLOTUS who served alongside their husbands. They all had the great honor of being the First Lady of the United States of America. They could have followed what their predecessors had done and gone down in history being called a duplication or copycat. What I saw instead, was each of them choosing to establish their unique causes with programs to implement change. This resulted in each of them forever standing out in history. Each FLOTUS, showed their individuality while in office and were influencers to their husbands in innumerable ways without being visible in those roles to the public.

This was so amazing to me and put the seal on our Genesis authority. God created man and then fashioned woman out of man—giving them both the authority to dominate and to rule. There was no competition with each other, nor was there comparisons of who was wittier, smarter, or who was the one that was large and in charge. The woman was part of man and the premiere designer, God, planned it that way.

Eve was the first mother, also, with no human motherly guide. I remember being a mother for the first time. I was so excited but had no clue what I was doing. I was going to rely on my mother's teachings, but there were plenty of new things I was going to learn firsthand. One day my cousin came over to visit and help me out with my new baby, and I just broke down crying. In between tears, I was saying I didn't know how to be a mother. That was my inadequacy and fear showing, and I was absolutely right.

Can you imagine how Eve, mother of all living, felt? She had no role model to look to or even try to remember what she saw growing up, no books on the matter that would serve as a quick study guide, no relatives to draw from. Being first can be a blessing and a curse. Because you are first in any category, be it a mother, eldest in the family, first lady of a church and so on, you get to set the standard, but you also have to blaze the trail feeling every emotion of anguish, the days and nights of fear of the unknown, the knocks and bumps that come along with setting the standard. When you set the standard, you have no idea whether what is being tracked is right or wrong. Eve didn't have a clue she was in a place to rule.

Here's one thing I do know. There was a plan drafted for us from the beginning—a Lamb was slain before the foundation of the world. God had a plan just in case Adam and Eve fell. The plan of redemption was then activated. Jesus Christ, our redeeming Savior, connected us back to our Genesis status. Genesis is a place of nothing being hidden, a place of authority and dominion and true intimacy with Father God. Eve, as well as every woman who has followed her, have been *Fashioned by God to Rule the World*. It's time for us all to rule.

Fashioned by God to Rule the World

Journal

Fashioned by God to Rule the World

Journal

Chapter 11
Eve's Loss of a Child

Elaine Robison

Elaine's HERstory

Elaine Robison, a gospel music psalmist under the leadership of the late Dr. D. Rayford Bell and now Bishop Warren Joel Hoard of Christ Temple Apostolic Faith Church, Inc. has ministered in song to God's people for more than forty years. Elaine's main purpose is to lift up the name of Jesus and to edify God's people through her ministry.

Elaine has toured nationally and internationally, carrying the message of the gospel through her power-packed music ministry. For three consecutive years she accepted an invitation from the US government to perform for our troops overseas in Kosovo, Macedonia, Bosnia and Germany. Her music ministry afforded her an opportunity to be one of the lead soloists for Rev. Dan Willis and the Pentecostals of Chicago. She also sang with Calvin Bridges and Chicago Praise, the group ENDOWED, and was once a lead singer for the Illinois State Council and PCAF National Mass choir.

She has traveled and recorded with the aforementioned groups, while yet faithfully working as a key Praise and Worship leader for her local assembly in the Chicagoland area. She has also carried her gift of praise to audiences via cable network TBN, and television broadcasts such as, *Ashes to Beauty*, the *Bobby Jones Show*, *Testify* and *I'm Just Saying* with Rev. Dan Willis. She was often called, "The Bootlegging Evangelist" because of her passion to bring the gospel of the Lord Jesus Christ to her audiences.

Elaine hosted the Gospel Brunch for the world-famous Chicago House of Blues establishment, for over fifteen years. She also performed at the Chicago Gospel Fest in Grant Park for two consecutive years and the International Christian Women's Conference and Christian Women in Media. She serves on the Board of Directors of Women of Vision and Destiny Ministries, Inc. as co-executive president and the Women in Worship psalmist. Additionally, she serves as president of Christ Temple's Sisterhood, and is also part of the Apostolic Jail & Prison Ministry.

Elaine was commissioned by God to take a step of faith as a soloist and now as an anointed and power-packed evangelist, sharing God's message at conferences, retreats and various events throughout the United States. God has blessed her to lift up His name and minister for His glory. Her performances are encouraging, uplifting and soul stirring; and her messages offer peace, joy, love and salvation through the Lord Jesus Christ. Her motto is, "If I can help somebody with the words of a song or a message, then my living will not be in vain."

Elaine has experienced some hardships along the way. As a child she had a terrible incident that almost took her life at the age of four. Growing up she experienced sexual abuse. Later in life, she thought she was marrying the love of her life, enduring an abusive relationship not once, but twice. After dealing with so much trauma it was through music, preaching and the grace of God that she was sustained. In 2006 she launched The Natalie Ford Project: Women Behind Bars, named after her daughter who passed away. Later, Elaine launched a prayer line for mothers to come together and pray for their children called #MIC Mothers Interceding for our Children.

Elaine is currently furthering her knowledge by attending the D.R. Bell Bible College.

Chapter 11
Eve's Loss of a Child

And Cain talked with Abel his brother: and it came to pass, when they were in the field, that Cain rose up against Abel his brother, and slew him.
—*Genesis 4:8*

How can you explain or even deal with the thought of losing a child? Everyone experiences loss and grieves differently. Some are able to go through the process of grieving and make it out, while others deal with deep depression and it looks as if they may not come out. But I'm here to tell you that there is hope and it is in Jesus! For those of you who have lost a child, I encourage you don't throw in the towel, help is here. And if you haven't lost a child, please read on as there may be something here that you can learn to help someone who has.

Romans 15:4 (NIV) says, "For everything that was written in the past was written to teach us, so that through the endurance taught in the Scriptures and the encouragement they provide we might have hope." The Scriptures do give us hope and encouragement as we wait patiently for God's promises to be fulfilled.

Let's go back to the beginning to the book of Genesis. In Hebrew, Genesis is *Bereshit*, which means, "is concerned with beginnings," and refers to the creation of the universe and the origin of humanity. This first book of the Bible quickly moves from universal history (Adam, Noah and Babel) to the history of Abraham, the first Jew. The remainder of the book focuses on the lives of the Jewish patriarchs, and especially the story of Joseph. The book ends with the entire family of Jacob migrating to Egypt to escape famine through the auspices of Joseph.

Fashioned by God to Rule the World

Hopefully you have already read the previous chapters, which give insight into where we are going. Let's look at our first family, Adam and Eve. We see in Genesis 2:18 (NIV) the Lord God said it is not good for the man Adam to be alone. I will make a helper suitable for him. God knew that Adam needed someone compatible, so He created Eve by taking a rib from Adam's side and fashioned her into His image, for purpose and with purpose. They were created equally but with different roles.

God's idea for creating women in this way makes us exceptional. We are special in the sight of God! After He created he him both male and female, he blessed them and commanded them to be fruitful and multiply and replenish the earth and subdue it. He wanted them to take authority over creation and rule over it. In other words, they were to fill the earth with godly offspring and glorify Him (God) through their rule on the earth (Psalm 8:5-6).

Together, Adam and Eve would fulfill God's purpose of populating the earth. How befitting it is for Eve, the first woman, to be also called the Mother of Life. She would have the responsibility of carrying out the nurturing duties of a mother who had no prior example to guide her through this process.

This leads us to Genesis 4, which opens up talking about Eve giving birth to her sons Cain and then Abel. It is here where we discover the first murder committed, and also the loss of her child. When Eve gave birth to her firstborn, she was so excited that she stated, "I have acquired a son from the Lord." Some commentaries said that she makes this statement because she may have thought that his was the seed that God was talking about in Genesis 3:16, when He was passing down the punishment for their disobedience. At that time, He told the serpent, "I will put enmity between thee and the woman and between thy seed and her seed; it shall bruise thy head, and thou shalt bruise his heel." She believed this, not knowing that this very son, Cain, would murder his brother, Abel.

Eve was the first woman to lose a child and the Bible doesn't really give us insight on how she felt or how she dealt with the loss of her son—actually she ended up losing both sons. I can imagine the pain and the hurt of not only losing a son, but knowing that it was her older son who murdered his brother. That is a lot to bear!

There was no other woman who was able to help her or give her encouragement or even support her during this difficult time. She had to go through this traumatic pain without a mother, sister, aunt, friend or support group. It was during this time that she needed divine help. She experienced the hand of God and His mercy toward her. He was not surprised about what happened; He already knew that Cain would take Abel's life. The God who is the God of all comfort, comforted her so that in the years to come we can look back and witness that God is able to comfort those who are going through their dark season. The scripture that comes to mind is in 2 Corinthians 1:3-4, the latter part of verse, "the God of all comfort; who comforteth us in all our tribulation, that we may be able to comfort them which are in any trouble, by the comfort wherewith we ourselves are comforted of God." That is a place to shout! Eve had to trust God's doing. And guess what? We have to trust Him too.

Losing a child is no easy thing. It plays on you mentally, emotionally, and physically. It leaves you asking questions, feeling like you did something wrong, and asking what you could have done to prevent the loss. Guilt moves in. It also makes you feel like you have been cheated out of the greatest experiences of your life. Not being able to see your child grow up or who they would have become or the things you would have done together is devastating. You're at a loss and there's so much going on in your mind until it can become completely overwhelming.

Let's visit the word "loss." It has several meanings, but I decided to highlight this one from Dictionary.com: the state or feeling of grief when deprived of someone or something of value. Losing a child is the most painful trauma any parent will ever experience. There's nothing that can compare to it. Parents are torn between trying to continue living, and loving those who are still here, while half of their heart is with their child who is gone. That's normal but we have to be careful. We have to give ourselves space to grieve over the loss of our child, but we cannot lose sight of our loved ones who are still living.

I'm quite sure Eve was experiencing all types of feelings. We must remember that she was the first mother to grieve the death of a son. She must have agonized over her son's crime of killing his brother. She must have felt the pain and shame of family estrangement. She likely had to work on rebuilding a marriage devastated by the grief of losing her sons. How in the world was she able to heal and move forward without the support of a mom, sister, or aunt? But God!

The bond between a mother and child is so powerful and when that bond is broken it is devastating. God has fashioned a woman so uniquely. He designed her body to carry another life. He uniquely created a womb to house the baby for nine months, allowing her to feel the joy of carrying a child and the movement of life on the inside, which creates that special bond between mom and baby. The feeling is indescribable.

God created us to be a wombed-man, designed to bear children. This house, the womb, is an astounding organ. Hundreds of years of medical technology and billions of dollars of research have proven unable to replicate it, let alone design one from scratch. We have learned how to conceive fetuses in test tubes, but we cannot grow them into children without a womb. A child that leaves this special place more than a few months before his time to be born, simply has no chance of surviving, unless God decides differently. Nothing is impossible with Him!

There is no such thing as an artificial womb. The uniqueness of the womb is a bit surprising, since at first glance, it doesn't seem to do all that much. But it is precisely the womb's quietness—its ability to be still, to listen, and to gently respond that is its genius. Modern science has revealed the womb to be an exquisitely sensitive organ, a vehicle that senses its occupant's every need, and tailors itself to accommodate that need.

It provides a precise and ever-changing balance of nutrients; it maintains perfectly calibrated pH levels; it discreetly disposes of toxins; it provides the right enzymes and antibodies at precisely the right times and in just the right doses. The biochemistry is complex and beyond imagination. A womb is not the work of humans. We could have never devised it. Through her womb, a woman encounters not just her child, but the Almighty Himself. In her creativity, she experiences the nearness of the Creator of All, the Master Designer.

According to *Eve Acquires a Son*, by Rabbi David Fohrma, if every woman who goes through childbirth is at least dimly aware of this mystery—if every woman, at least to some extent, senses the "science-fiction-like" quality of childbirth—think of how Eve must have felt. What she went through didn't just seem utterly new and unprecedented. It *was* utterly new and unprecedented. This was the first human birth in history. No one had ever been through this before. She must have seen herself as part of a miracle beyond imagining.

The awesomeness of God is shown through the miraculous events that happen every time a child is born. So, to lose a child or children is unbelievable. But there is life after loss. God never intended for this tragedy to take you out, or to hurt you. There is purpose behind every pain, every hurt and every tragic circumstance that we may experience. We have to know what it is and trust God. His Word tells us to trust in the Lord with all our heart and lean not to our own understanding (Proverbs 3:5).

I feel the need to share my own story. It's one of pain, hurt, not understanding, asking why me or what could I have done to prevent this, thinking that she's my only child and we'll never be able to do things together again like shopping, going to church and praising God together. Hopefully this will encourage you, and let you know that you can make it, not by just existing but with purpose in your life, living the life that God has called you to live.

For some reason God allowed me to go through the loss of a child. I would hear people say if God brought you to it, He can bring you through it. 1 Corinthians 10:13 tells us, "There hath no temptation taken you but such as is common to man: but God *is* faithful, who will not suffer you to be tempted above that ye are able; but will with the temptation also make a way to escape, that ye may be able to bear *it*." I'm sharing the Word because it was the Word that brought me through this terrible time.

This was my only biological child, and we wanted a girl so badly. She would be my mother's first grandchild. We both wanted a girl so that we could dress her in bows and beautiful dresses. God allowed me to give birth to a baby girl who weighed more than seven pounds. My heart was so overjoyed. During the pregnancy we experienced a few things. But God! Who would ever think that life would abruptly end for her at age twenty-nine? No pain that I had ever experienced could compare to this pain. I lost my biological father, my stepfather and my mother, but the pain I felt with those losses did not compare.

It's not normal for parents to bury their children, the children are supposed to bury the parents. But God had another plan for her life and mine. In this day and time, we are experiencing death of all ages more frequently than before. It's nothing new because throughout the Bible mothers lost their children. When you are going through it you feel like, how can I bear this?

The loss of my daughter was greater than any pain I have ever known! It was during this time that I got to know God on a whole different level. The scripture in Hebrews 13:5 (AMP) breaks it down like this, "For He has said, 'I will never (under any circumstances) desert you (nor give you up nor leave you without support, nor will I in any degree leave you helpless), nor will I forsake or let you down or relax my hold on you (assuredly not)!'"

  I'm a living witness that God did not leave me nor forsake me. As a matter of fact, He allowed me to experience some miraculous things during this time. He allowed me to spend six weeks with my daughter before He took her home. Her numbers were good, which confused the doctor. She had stated before passing away that she was going home. Nobody picked up what she meant, thinking she was speaking naturally. But she was speaking in the Spirit that she was going home to be with the Lord. On the day that she passed, I got a chance to see her transition take place, her countenance change. Still, I didn't understand until we got the call that Monday at 10:00 pm that she was gone. But the Lord didn't leave me there.

  I was in so much pain and unable to process that she was gone, I couldn't go to the hospital to see her that night. I just couldn't face it. The next morning, we all went to the hospital to view her body. This is where the Lord began to show Himself mighty. After arriving at the hospital, we were told that we had to wait to view her body, because the staff was very busy. So, we were getting ready to sit and wait. After a few minutes, a lady came to me and asked if I was ready to go see my daughter in the morgue. I replied yes, so she led us down the hall. We discovered this woman had no name on her tag. She began to talk to me and assure me that I needed to trust God. She stated that Nikki didn't look the way she looked when I saw her that Monday. The men who were in the morgue were not dressed as security guards, as they should have been. After leaving the viewing room, the woman talked with us and left. As we were leaving the building two nurses and a chaplain came to escort us to the morgue. When I told them what had happened, that we'd already been taken back to see my daughter, they looked confused. They asked me a few questions and we left.

When we got home my husband began to analyze what had happened. We came to the conclusion that in the hospital morgue, we were in the presence of angels. I could go on and on about the miraculous power of our Lord. Even after the funeral the Lord continued to sustain me and keep my heart encouraged. I have my days, but I realize that the Lord is my strength. One thing I never stated out of my mouth is that I can't make it. I've never spoken negative words regarding my daughter's death. Our words have power. Death and life are in the power of your tongue.

One day I will be able to share the whole story, but through her death I've been able to encourage other mothers who have lost their child or children. I let them know that there is life after the death of your child. You have a choice. It's a process, but God, who is rich in mercy has already made a way for you to make it! We have someone who understands our hurts and our pains.

Hebrews 4:16 (AMP) says, *"For we do not have a High Priest who is unable to sympathize and understand our weaknesses and temptations, but One who has been tempted (knowing exactly how it feels to be human) in every respect as we are, yet without [committing any] sin."*

At the end of Genesis 4 we see a spark in Eve's story. She says in verse twenty-five that God has granted me another child in place of Abel, since Cain killed him. According to David Guzik's Bible Commentary, Adam and Eve had many children who were not specifically named in the biblical record, but Seth was worthy of mention because he, in some sense, replaced Abel and was the one to whom the promise of a deliverer from the seed of the woman (Genesis 3:15) would be passed.

God restored and healed Eve. This is not to say that she got over the loss of her son, but she was able to move on and live after her loss.

Fashioned by God to Rule the World

Journal

Journal

Fashioned by God to Rule the World

Enjoy more books by the

Rich Gurlz Club Inc.

Available

amazon

Fashioned by God to Rule the World

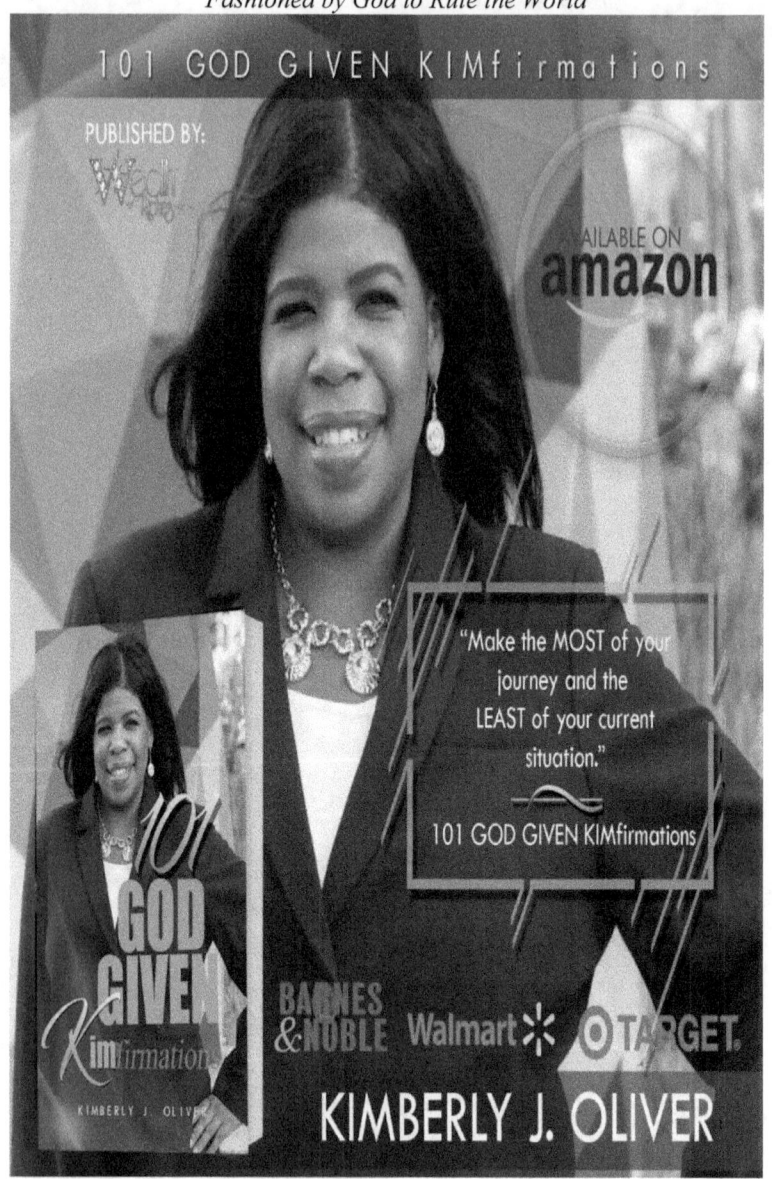

Fashioned by God to Rule the World

10 KEYS TO TURN YOUR POT OF OIL INTO AN OIL FIELD

THE Widow OIL Tycoon ™

AVAILABLE ON amazon

BILLIONAIRE VISIONNAIRE

L Renee Richardson ™ MBA

L. RENEE HAS BEEN FEATURED IN

Fashioned by God to Rule the World

Fashioned by God to Rule the World

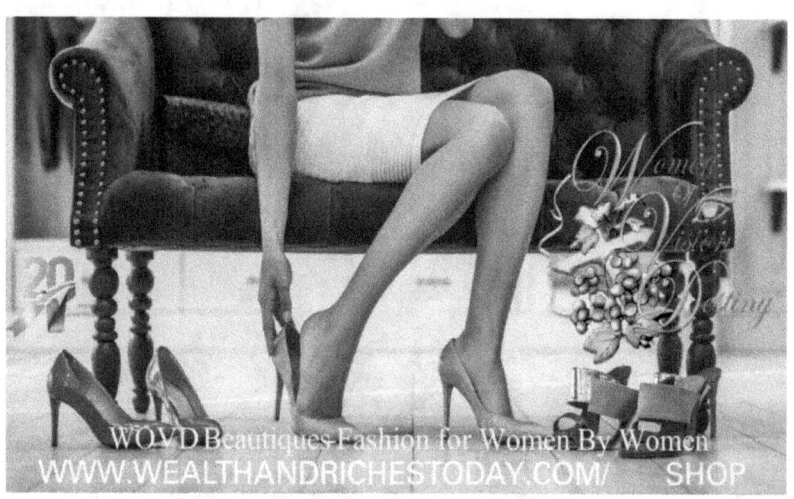

Fashioned by God to Rule the World

www.ingramcontent.com/pod-product-compliance
Lightning Source LLC
Chambersburg PA
CBHW070939240426
43667CB00036B/2391